IMMANUEL KANT

IMMANUEL KANT

A very brief history

ANTHONY KENNY

First published in Great Britain in 2019

Society for Promoting Christian Knowledge
36 Causton Street
London SW1P 4ST
www.spck.org.uk

British Library Cataloguing-in-Publication Data
A catalogue record for this book is available from the British Library

ISBN 978–0–281–07654–3
eBook ISBN 978–0–281–07655–0

1 3 5 7 9 10 8 6 4 2

Typeset by Manila Typesetting Company
Printed in Great Britain by Ashford Colour Press

eBook by Manila Typesetting Company

Produced on paper from sustainable forests

For Nancy

Contents

Contents

Part 2
THE LEGACY

Preface

In 2017 SPCK published my book on the Enlightenment in the Very Brief History series. The publisher originally proposed that the volume should include a chapter on Kant. I responded that Kant was too great a figure to be treated merely as a member of a movement, and that moreover as the father of German idealism he helped to bring the Enlightenment to an end. The publisher's response was to invite me to contribute a second volume in the series, devoted solely to Kant. That is how the present book came to be written.

I am indebted to those who read the text in draft, and who suggested corrections and improvements: notably Nancy Kenny, Peter Hacker, Jill Paton Walsh, Philip Law, Brian Davies and Steve Gove. It would be rash to say that all remaining errors are my own work, since many of them will have been copied from other writers. But they are, of course, my responsibility.

Anthony Kenny

Abbreviations and conventions

All references to Kant's works are to the English translations of his works in *The Cambridge Edition of the Works of Immanuel Kant* (Cambridge University Press, 1993–), cited by volume and page. The volumes of this edition contain in the margin the page numbers of the German originals in the Deutsche Akademie der Wissenschaften edition, *Kants gesammelte Schriften* (Berlin, 1900–). As similar marginal references are now standardly included in English translations, it is easy by means of these to move from the Cambridge reference to other versions to which the reader may have access.

The works of Kant cited in this book are included in five of the Cambridge volumes:

> *The Only Possible Argument in Support of the Existence of God, Dreams of a Spirit-Seer* and *False Subtlety* are contained in *Theoretical Philosophy 1755–1770*, ed. David Walford and Ralf Meerbote (CUP, 1992). Cited as WM followed by page number;
>
> *Critique of Pure Reason* is in a single volume edited by Paul Guyer and Allen Wood (CUP, 1998). Cited as CPR plus page number;
>
> *Groundwork of the Metaphysics of Morals, Critique of Practical Reason, Toward Perpetual Peace* and *The Metaphysics of Morals* are contained in the volume *Practical Philosophy*, ed. Mary Gregor (CUP, 1996). Cited as GM plus page number;

Critique of the Power of Judgment is in a single volume
  edited by Paul Guyer and Eric Matthews (CUP, 2000).
  Cited as CPJ plus page number;
Religion within the Boundaries of Mere Reason is included
  in the volume *Religion and Rational Theology*, trans.
  and ed. Allen Wood and George di Giovanni (CUP,
  1996). Cited as WG plus page number.

The Cambridge translations are reliable but they are not
always elegant. They adhere closely to Kant's syntax, thereby
producing sentences that are intolerably long in translation.
Also, they make use of some hideous neologisms, such as
'cognize' instead of 'know'. I am greatly indebted to the
Cambridge versions, but have felt free to adapt them from
time to time to make things easier for the English reader.

Chronology

Part 1

THE HISTORY

1

Kant's early life

Immanuel Kant was born in 1724 in the town of Königsberg near the eastern coast of the Baltic. A thriving centre of international trade, Königsberg was then part of the young kingdom of Prussia, which was just beginning its long competition with Austria to become the leading German-speaking nation. The town has now changed its name to Kaliningrad and sits in an enclave of the Russian federation, rarely visited by foreigners except when Russia is hosting the World Cup.

Kant's father was a master harness maker, prominent in the local guild. He brought up the young Immanuel as a Lutheran. Among Luther's main doctrines were that the human race was so corrupt by nature that it was impossible for a human being to keep all the commandments of God; and that it was only through faith in the merits of Jesus that a human being could be saved by the grace of God. The first of these doctrines, but not the second, remained a lifelong strand in Kant's thought.

The Kant family belonged to a distinctively devout group of Lutherans known as Pietists. In later life Immanuel acknowledged a debt to the seriousness of the moral education he had received at home, though he disliked the introverted religiosity of the Pietist school to which he was sent.

During the years when Kant was at school two events stand out. In 1737 his mother died at the age of 40, having

3

caught smallpox while on an errand of mercy to a sick friend. Three years later King Frederick William I of Prussia died, leaving the throne to his son, the future Frederick the Great. The new king was a paragon of enlightenment in the study and a ruthless aggressor on the battlefield. It was during his 46-year reign that Kant's major works were written.

In 1740 Kant entered the town's university, the Albertina. He was by all accounts a sober and industrious scholar, lacking both the means and the inclination for the excesses of his fellow students. In philosophy the dominant influence in the university was the thought of Leibniz, as codified by his acquaintance Christian Wolff. The professor of logic and metaphysics, Martin Knutzen, instructed Kant in the intricacies of the Wolffian system. More importantly, he allowed his pupil the use of his own copious scientific library and awoke his interest in the physics and astronomy of Isaac Newton.

In 1746 the death of Kant's father left him responsible for the upkeep of two sisters and a brother. He left Königsberg and for the next seven or eight years was a tutor to various families in nearby villages. His last post was with the family of Count Kaiserlingk, whose wife was a philosophy enthusiast who had translated Wolff into French. Kant found time to write a book, *The Estimation of Living Forces*, which was an attempt to mediate in a debate between René Descartes and G. W. Leibniz about the measurement of force. It was published in German, not Latin, and was not submitted to the university as a dissertation.

In 1754 Kant returned to Königsberg and shortly after submitted a doctoral thesis on the topic of fire (*De Igne*). He still had 15 years to wait before being appointed to a professorship. During this period he earned his living by lecturing as a *Privatdozent*. Holding forth on many scientific topics as well as on philosophy, he became a popular and indeed witty lecturer, inserting jokes and funny stories into set texts. Initially poor, he refused to allow his friends to buy him a new coat when his old one wore out; but after a few years he was prosperous enough to become a generous host and something of a dandy. However he was not rich enough, in his own estimate, to marry, in spite of his fondness for the company of women.

Kant continued to publish on scientific subjects. The most significant work of this period is his 1755 *General Natural History and Theory of the Heavens*. According to this, matter was created by God but initially lacked motion, which was produced by the natural forces of attraction and repulsion. The development of the universe from an initial state took millions of years, and will continue for ever. Our solar system arose when a cloud of material around the sun contracted and fragmented into a plane. This nebular theory was independently given magisterial mathematical formulation at the end of the eighteenth century by the French astronomer Laplace.

In 1758, in the course of the Seven Years War, Russian soldiers occupied Königsberg, where they remained for nearly five years. The occupation seems to have made little difference to Kant's life, and he lectured to, and dined with, Russian officers. When in due course the Russians left, Kant was happy to give tutorials to the Prussian officers who replaced them, and their General Meyer became his regular dining companion.

In this period, Kant's philosophical position was undergoing radical change. The influence of Wolff was replaced by those of David Hume (whose *Inquiry Concerning Human Understanding* had appeared in German in 1755) and Jean-Jacques Rousseau (whose *Discourse on Inequality* appeared in the same year). Kant later acquired an engraved portrait of Rousseau, the only picture he ever possessed. Meanwhile, younger German philosophers came to sit at his feet. J. G. Hamann, a disenchanted child of the Enlightenment, complained that in order to get into Kant's 7 a.m. lecture it was important to arrive an hour earlier. The romantic philosopher J. C. Herder wrote that in his lectures Kant 'though in the prime of life, still had the joyful high spirits of a young man, which he kept, I believe, into extreme old age'. Herder's notes on Kant's lectures have survived and exhibit the influence of Rousseau.

It would be another 11 years before Kant produced the work on which his fame principally rests, the *Critique of Pure Reason*. But already in this pre-critical period, while still only a private lecturer, he published in 1762 a work that is still worth close examination: *The Only Possible Argument in Support of the Existence of God*.

2

Early natural theology

Throughout his life, Kant believed in the existence of a personal God who was the wise governor of the universe, and he thought it necessary that everyone should share the same belief. He changed his mind over time, however, as to the best way of reaching and supporting that belief. He also varied in his attitude to the proofs of God's existence that had been offered by previous philosophers. In his earliest venture in this area, *The Only Possible Argument in Support of the Existence of God*, he offers what appears to be a proof of the divine existence. He does not claim that it is a demonstration, by which he seems to mean a proof presented in syllogistic form and involving the rigorous definition of terms. Undoubtedly, though, he felt that his work prepared the way for such a demonstrative proof. But he warns us that the task involves a venture into the depths of metaphysics – 'a dark ocean without coasts and without lighthouses' (WM, 111).

Kant divides would-be proofs of God's existence into two classes: those that start from experience of the actual world, and those that start from concepts of the merely possible. He names the former 'cosmological arguments' and the latter 'ontological arguments'. The best-known cosmological arguments – though Kant does not mention them – are St Thomas Aquinas' Five Ways. The best-known ontological argument is Descartes' claim that since God contains all

7

perfections, and existence is a perfection, God must exist. Kant devotes much energy to exposing the weakness of this proof.

The key point of his criticism is that existence is not a predicate. Consider, he says, all the predicates that are true of Julius Caesar. 'Combine in him all his conceivable predicates, not even excluding those of time and place, and you will quickly see that with all of these determinations he can exist or not exist' (WM, 117). Of course it is natural to say that lions exist and unicorns do not; but what that really means is that among the things that exist, some fall under the concept *lion* but none falls under the concept *unicorn*.

We can use the word 'is' in two different ways. If we say 'God is omnipotent' we are simply coupling a predicate to a subject: an atheist can agree that omnipotence is a property of the God whose existence he denies. If we say 'there is a God' we are doing something different: Kant calls this 'positing'. To posit God is to state that he exists. Kant warns us, however, that saying 'God is an existing thing' is misleading; the more accurate expression is 'Something existent is God', or even more precisely 'Those predicates taken together that we signify by the expression "God" belong to an existent thing.'

If existence is not a predicate at all, then it is certainly not a predicate indicating a perfection, and so Descartes' argument that existence must belong to the most perfect being falls to the ground. But Kant goes on to offer a different argument from 'possible being', an argument which therefore by his definition counts as ontological. Kant's ontological argument goes as follows.

First we must distinguish between logical possibility and real possibility. A square circle is logically impossible because there is a contradiction between the notions of *square* and *circle*. A right-angled triangle is logically possible because there is no corresponding contradiction involved. But it is not only logically but also really possible, or as Kant sometimes puts it, materially possible: 'The triangle as well as the right angle are the data or the material of this possible thing' (WM, 123).

We next ask whether it is possible that nothing whatever exists. This seems to be logically possible, since the hypothesis contains no internal contradiction. But real possibility depends upon the presence of data or material, and if all existence is denied, then no such data or material are available. Thus, if all existence is denied, there is no real possibility, and if anything is to be possible something must be actual.

There must be something which is not only actual, Kant goes on to argue: it must also be necessary.

> All possibility presupposes something actual in which and through which everything conceivable is given. Accordingly there is a certain actuality whose removal would take away all internal possibility. But something whose removal or negation destroys all possibility is absolutely necessary. Accordingly there is something that exists in an absolutely necessary fashion. (WM, 127)

Kant goes on to argue that the necessary being must be single, simple, immutable, eternal, spiritual, and indeed possess all the attributes of God. There is no need to follow these later details of his argument because already at this point it can be seen to be flawed. From the premise 'Every possibility necessarily supposes some actuality' Kant draws the conclusion 'Every possibility supposes something that is necessarily actual'. But this is a fallacious move which starts from a true premise to arrive at a dubious conclusion.

Consider a parallel case. In a knockout competition, such as the Wimbledon tennis tournament, if there are to be any winners, then necessarily there are to be some losers. But this does not mean that there are some people who are necessarily losers. Whether any individual player is a winner or a loser depends on how he or she plays on the day. This shows how the placement of the word 'necessarily' may make all the difference between a valid and an invalid argument.

In the second and third sections of the book, Kant turns to the arguments which at this point in his life he calls 'cosmological'. He devotes most attention to the claim that the existence of purpose in the world means that it is the product of an intelligent designer. He has – and will retain through his life – a great respect for this contention, and he is willing to concede that there are countless structures in nature whose immediate ground must be the final intention of their creator. He himself is anxious to engage in what he calls 'physico-theology' – the method of ascending from observations of nature to the knowledge of God. He is indeed anxious to stress the limitations of current physico-theology, but with the aim of strengthening it rather than undermining it.

First, Kant points out that it is wrong to think that if some element or structure is useful to humans, that utility must have been what motivated its designer. Water tends to hold itself level; it is absurd to suggest that this is in order that humans can mirror themselves in it. The moons of Jupiter are useful to navigators with telescopes, but were they created only to give men a handy means of ascertaining their longitude?

Second, there is no need to invoke the intention of a designer when purely mechanical causes suffice to explain a phenomenon. Kant imagines a designer who wishes the coasts of tropical countries to have a bearable climate. He accordingly invents a sea breeze. But it will not do for this wind to blow at night as well as in the daytime. So he must devise a mechanism to arrange for seaward winds to return in the middle of the night. But one might worry about the further consequences of any such device. Any such worry, Kant suggests, is foolish. 'What good providence would order on the basis of considered choice, the air itself performs according to the universal laws of motion' (WM, 141).

Appeal to the immediate ordering of providence is often just a lazy way of avoiding research into the immediate causes of phenomena. To show the way in which such research should be carried out, Kant sketches accounts of the origin of mountains and of the construction of river channels on this earth, and also of the source and motions of the heavenly bodies in the solar system. His scientific writing, though inevitably superannuated in some respects, is always well informed and insightful.

Kant emphasizes that the attempt to explain effects by the operation of mechanical causes rather than by the voluntary fiat of a designer in no way diminishes the value of the argument from design. Indeed he thinks it has a greater appeal than his own ontological argument from possibility. It is inadequate, however, as a proof of the existence of God, because it leads not to a creator but to an architect: a superhuman intelligence that gives the world system, order and teleology.

3

Kant the professor

In 1763 the Berlin Academy set as a prize question 'whether metaphysical truths can be demonstrated with the same certainty as truths of geometry'. Kant's (unsuccessful) entry for the prize underlined a number of crucial distinctions between mathematical and philosophical method. Mathematicians, he said, start from clear definitions which create concepts which they then develop; philosophers start from confused concepts and analyse them in order to reach a definition. Metaphysicians, rather than aping mathematicians, should follow Newtonian methods, but should apply them not to the physical world but to the phenomena of inner experience.

In his enthusiasm for Newtonian science, and in his own early scientific writings, Kant showed himself in sympathy with the ideals of the thinkers of the French Enlightenment, such as Voltaire and the contributors to the great *Encyclopédie* which appeared between 1751 and 1766. He shared their belief in scientific progress, but he was also aware of its dangers. In 1762 he wrote:

> Ours is an age in which things which are worth knowing are increasing in number. It will not be long before our ability grows too weak and our lives too short for us to be able to understand even the most useful of these things.
>
> (WM, 100)

In 1765 Kant made friends with an English merchant, Joseph Green, an austere bachelor with whom he discussed the works of Hume and Rousseau. His life, always regular, now became more punctual: it was said that the housewives of the city would set their clocks by the time at which he left Green's house. In 1766 he became sub-librarian of the university; the additional earnings enabled him to move into new premises in the house of his publisher, which included a lecture room, a bookstore and a coffee house.

It was when he was appointed professor of logic and metaphysics in 1770 that Kant's income finally became satisfactory, and the promotion also gave him a lighter teaching load. But he still had to lecture every day, starting at 7 a.m. Having hired a retired soldier to wake him each day at five, after rising he would meditate for two hours over tea and a pipe. When the lecture was over he would write until it was time for lunch. This he always took in company, providing each of his guests with a pint of red wine, and finishing the meal with a round of jokes, on the ground that laughter was good for the digestion. Then came the time for a solitary walk, prior to the daily conversation with Green.

When he began his professorship, Kant's philosophical opinions seem to have been poised between the rationalist metaphysics of Leibniz and the empiricist scepticism of Hume. During the 1760s he had become increasingly sceptical of the possibility of a scientific metaphysics. The skittish *Dreams of a Spirit-Seer*, published anonymously in 1766, compared metaphysical speculations with the esoteric fantasies of the visionary Immanuel Swedenborg. Among other things the work emphasized, as Hume had done, that causal relations could be known only through experience and were never matters of logical necessity.

This work later embarrassed Kant, but it contained the germs of some of his later ideas. Consider, for instance, the following reflections on the nature of morality:

> Can that person really be called honest, can he really be called virtuous, who would readily abandon himself to his favourite vices, were it not for the deterrence of future punishment? . . .

> There has never existed, I suppose, an upright soul which was capable of supporting the thought that with death everything was at an end, and whose noble disposition has not aspired to the hope that there would be a future. For this reason, it seems more consonant with human nature and moral purity to base the expectation of a future world on the sentiments of a nobly constituted soul, than, conversely, to base its noble conduct on the hope of another world.
>
> (WM, 359)

Having turned down a call to a chair of poetry a few years earlier, in 1770 Kant was appointed professor of logic and metaphysics at Königsberg. Despite the sceptical elements of the works of the 1760s, his inaugural dissertation as professor (*On the Form and Principles of the Sensory and Intellectual World*) still shows the strong influence of Leibniz. Like Leibniz, he denied that all our concepts are derived from the senses, and like Leibniz he believed that in addition to the sensory world there is an intellectual world. He did not, however, accept Leibniz's claim that the material world is ultimately constituted by the simple, immaterial, independent elements Leibniz called monads.

During the 1770s Kant worked silently on developing his own metaphysical system. The slow progress of the work can be followed in the optimistic letters he wrote to his friends in the 1770s in which he announced that he was nearing the completion of an entirely new conceptual science. Writing to Marcus Herz in 1773 he expressed the hope that by the following Easter he would have succeeded in giving philosophy a durable form, and 'an appearance that will make her attractive to shy mathematicians so that they may regard her pursuit as both possible and respectable'. But as the decade ended, he had not yet produced a publishable work.

4

Kant's Copernican revolution

The 1780s were a remarkable period in human history, in which Gibbon was publishing his *Decline and Fall of the Roman Empire*, Boswell was writing his *Life of Johnson*, Turner began to exhibit in the Royal Academy, and Mozart composed *The Marriage of Figaro* and *Don Giovanni*. Early in the decade the United States received its constitution, and before it ended the French Revolution had taken place. Among the seminal events of the decade was the publication of Kant's *Critique of Pure Reason*, first in 1781 and in a revised edition in 1787.

Kant's aim was to make philosophy, for the first time, fully scientific. Mathematics had been scientific for many centuries, and since Bacon, Descartes and Newton scientific physics had come of age. But metaphysics, the oldest discipline, the one which 'would survive even if all the rest were swallowed up in the abyss of an all-destroying barbarism', was still far from maturity. Metaphysical curiosity was inherent in human nature: human beings could not but be interested in the three main objects of metaphysics, namely God, freedom and immortality. But could metaphysics become a true science?

It could do so, Kant claimed, only if philosophy underwent a revolution similar to that which Copernicus had achieved for physics when he placed the sun, rather than the earth, at the centre of the solar system. Copernicus had shown that when we think we are observing the motion of the sun round the earth what we see is the consequence of the rotation of our own earth. The revolution Kant proposed would do for our intellect what Copernicus did for our vision. Instead of asking how our knowledge can conform to its objects, he said, we must start from the supposition that objects must conform to our thinking. Only in this way can we justify the claim of metaphysics to possess knowledge that is necessary and universal.

Kant distinguishes between two modes of knowledge: knowledge *a priori* and knowledge *a posteriori*. We know a truth *a posteriori* if we know it through experience; we know it *a priori* if we know it independently of all experience. There are some things that we know *a priori*, fundamental truths that are not mere generalizations from experience: the truths of mathematics provide obvious examples. Among the judgements that we make *a priori* some, Kant says, are analytic and some are synthetic. In an analytic judgement, such as 'all bodies are extended', we are merely making explicit in the predicate something that is already contained in the concept of the subject. But in a synthetic judgement the predicate adds something to the content of the subject: Kant's example is 'all bodies are heavy'. All *a posteriori* propositions are synthetic, and all analytic propositions are *a priori*. Can there be propositions that are synthetic, and yet *a priori*?

Kant believes that there can. Arithmetic and geometry are synthetic because they go beyond pure logic, and yet they are *a priori* because they are known independently of experience. For him, therefore, mathematics offers examples of synthetic *a priori* truths. Most importantly, he claims that there must be propositions that are both *a priori* and synthetic if it is ever going to be possible to make a genuine science out of metaphysics. How synthetic *a priori* propositions are possible is therefore the principal problem for philosophy.

In addressing this problem the philosopher's first task is to make plain the nature and limits of the powers of the mind. Ever since his doctoral dissertation Kant had made a sharp distinction between the senses and the intellect: sensory knowledge is knowledge of objects as they appear, intellectual knowledge is knowledge of things as they are. Now he goes on to contrast the intellect (*Verstand*) with the faculty of reason (*Vernunft*). The intellect operates in combination with the senses in order to provide human knowledge: through the senses, objects are given us, through the intellect they are made thinkable. Experience has a content, provided by the senses, and a structure, determined by the intellect:

> For human knowledge, both senses and intellect are necessary.
>
> Neither of these faculties has a priority over the other. Without the senses no object would be given to us, and without the intellect no object could be thought. Thoughts without content are empty, awareness without concepts is blind . . . The understanding is aware of nothing, the senses can think nothing. Only through their union can knowledge arise.　　　　　　　　　　　　　　(CPR, 193)

Reason, by contrast with intellect, is the human mind's endeavour to go beyond what intellect can achieve. When divorced from experience it is 'pure reason', and it is that which is the target of Kant's critique.

Before addressing pure reason, Kant's *Critique* makes a systematic study of the senses and the intellect. The senses are studied in a section entitled 'Transcendental aesthetic' and the intellect in a section entitled 'Transcendental logic'. 'Transcendental' is a favourite word of Kant's; he used it in several different senses, but common to all of them is the notion of something which (for better or worse) goes beyond and behind the deliverances of actual experience. 'Aesthetic' here does not have its usual meaning, common already in Kant's day, of the study of the beautiful and the sublime. It simply means the study of human sense experience.

5

The transcendental aesthetic

A sense faculty such as sight or smell is, according to Kant, in itself no more than a passive power of receiving representations. However, sense provides only the matter of our experience, that is to say what makes the difference between a flash of light and a patch of dark, or between the smell of a rose and the smell of a cheese. Considered in itself the matter of sensation exhibits only chaos; it is the intellect that brings order into this manifold by classifying items under one or more concepts. The very notions of light and dark, of rose and cheese, are contributed not by the senses but by the intellect. Any object of sense is necessarily also an object of thought.

In his transcendental aesthetic Kant tries to isolate sense-experience as an object of study by stripping off all that is contributed by the intellect. He asks whether the form of experience is derived entirely from the concepts of the intellect, or whether some part of it is due to the nature of sensation itself. He answers that it will be found that there are two pure forms of sensory awareness, serving as principles of *a priori* knowledge, namely space and time. Space is the form of the outer senses which apprehend the world around us, time is the form of the inner sense by which the mind is aware of its own successive states.

It is easy to accept that any experience must be bound by space and time: it must occur somewhere, and it must occur somewhen. Even the simplest and most basic record of experience must have a form similar to 'here, now, dark'; and the 'here' and 'now' of such a protocol link into a network of other places and other times. But are the space and time that provide the form of experience something real in themselves, or are they merely creations of our own faculties?

It seems that we can know truths about space and time that are based on sensory awareness (because they are not analytic) and yet *a priori* (because they are prior to any experience). Kant argues that the knowledge of synthetic *a priori* truths about space and time is only explicable if they are forms of experience rather than properties of things in themselves. Empirically space and time are real, but transcendentally they are ideal. If we take away every subject, space and time disappear: these as phenomena cannot exist in themselves but only in us.

We normally distinguish between appearance and reality, assigning the rainbow to the former, and the raindrops to the latter. If we look more closely, Kant says, not only the drops of rain, but even their round shape and the space in which they fall, are only appearances, modifications of our sensory awareness.

What are we to make of this contention? We may readily grant that the measurement of space and time are activities of the mind. Metres and seconds are human creations. But does that mean that order in space and time is a feature of our experience rather than an objective reality? Surely it is a simple matter of fact whether the sun is larger than the earth, and whether the Battle of Hastings came before or after the defeat of the Spanish Armada.

During his lifetime, Kant offered no convincing response to this claim. Whether it is true or false will be best considered when, at the end of this book, we consider what has happened to the philosophy of space and time in the centuries succeeding his death.

6

The deduction of the categories

Fundamental to Kant's theory of human knowledge is the thesis that knowledge is possible only through the union of sense and intellect. Accordingly, having given an account of the senses in the transcendental aesthetic, he goes on to offer a transcendental logic which is an account of the intellect, the creative part of the mind. By 'logic' he tells us he means 'the absolutely necessary rules of thought without which there can be no employment whatever of the intellect'. He is not interested in the origin or history of our thoughts; that would be a matter for anthropology rather than logic.

Kant's project of delineating the boundaries of human understanding falls into two parts, one positive and one negative. The positive part sets out the criteria for the valid empirical employment of the intellect: this part of the transcendental logic is called 'the transcendental analytic'. The negative part offers a critique of the illusory dogmatic employment of the reason: this is called 'the transcendental dialectic'.

The intellect itself operates in two different stages. The intellect proper is the power to form concepts; the faculty of judgement is the power to apply concepts. A concept is in fact nothing other than the power to make judgements of certain kinds. The operations of the intellect find expression in individual words, the operations of the judging faculty find expression in whole sentences. For instance, to possess the concept *animal* is to have the power to make judgements containing the word 'animal' or some equivalent.

In his analytic Kant considers both concepts and judgements, in each case trying to sort out the empirical from the transcendental elements. He lays out a set of *a priori* concepts which he calls 'categories', and a set of *a priori* judgements which he calls 'principles'. Accordingly, the transcendental analytic is again subdivided into two main sections, containing 'the deduction of the categories' and 'the system of principles'.

What is meant by all this terminology? We may start with the notion of 'category'. It is easy enough to group concepts, and the predicates that express them, into classes. 'Blue' and 'green' obviously belong in the class of colour-predicates, 'square' and 'oval' in the class of shape-predicates. These, however, are low-level groupings: each of them might be subsumed into a higher-level classification such as 'quality' and 'quantity'. Kant wants to see whether all concepts and predicates can be grouped into some fundamental, necessary classes; such a class is what he calls a 'category'. As instances of such categories, Kant offers the concepts of 'cause' and 'substance'. Without these categories, he argues, we could not conceptualize or understand even the most fragmentary and disordered experience.

A substantial proportion of the transcendental analytic is devoted to the deduction, or legitimation, of the categories. By the deduction of a concept, Kant means a proof that we have a title to use it, a proof that in using it we are acting within our epistemological rights. If the concept to be deduced is an *a priori* one, then its deduction cannot be a mere empirical explanation of how we acquired it. The proof has to be 'transcendental', that is to say it must show that the concept is necessary if there is to be any such thing as experience at all.

Because concepts are powers to make judgement, Kant takes the starting point of his deduction from the different kinds of judgement. There are many different kinds of judgement: they may, for instance, be universal or particular judgements (using 'all' v. 'some'), affirmative or negative judgements (without or with a 'not'). More importantly, as Kant illustrates by examples, they may be categorical ('there is a perfect justice') or hypothetical ('if there is a perfect justice, the obstinately wicked are punished') or disjunctive ('the world exists either through blind chance, or through inner necessity, or through an external cause').

Corresponding to the different kinds of judgement there are different fundamental types of concepts. Kant seeks to relate each category to a different kind of judgement. For instance, he relates the category of substance to unqualified judgements, the category of cause to hypothetical judgements, and the category of interaction to disjunctive judgements. The specific links he makes are not always convincing, but we cannot deny the importance of the general claim that there are some concepts that are indispensable if anything is to count as the operation of intellect. Is the claim true?

If we think of the human intellect as consisting basically in the ability to master language, we may put Kant's question into linguistic form. Are there any concepts that must find expression in any fully fledged language? The answer seems to be that any genuine language-users, however alien they may be to us, need to have a concept of negation, and the ability to use quantifiers such as 'all' and 'some'. These are the concepts corresponding to Kant's distinction between affirmative and negative judgements, and his distinction between universal and particular judgements. Again, any rational language-user will need the ability to draw conclusions from premises, and this ability is expressed in the mastery of words like 'if', 'then' and 'therefore', which are related to Kant's class of hypothetical judgements. So, however unconvincing details of the transcendental deduction of the categories may be, it seems correct to link concepts with judgements and to claim that certain concepts must be fundamental to all understanding.

But what of the specific categories that Kant deduces? One of them is the concept of 'cause'. If the concept is *a priori* then experience cannot be cited as its origin. Kant accepts Hume's claim that experience could never prove the necessity and universality of the link between cause and effect. For all experience can tell us, the world might be such a chaos that no such link could ever be established. The thrust of the transcendental deduction is that if we did not have the categories, including the category of cause, we could not make sense of anything, we could not conceptualize even the most fragmentary and disordered experience.

Three elements are involved in the conceptualization of experience. First, items of sensory awareness are ordered in time; second, they are united in a single consciousness; and finally, the conscious subject brings them under concepts.

It is not possible for me to *discover* that something is an item of *my* consciousness. I cannot be, as it were, faced with an item of consciousness, go on to wonder to whom it belongs, and conclude, upon inquiry, that it belongs to none other than myself. I can, through reflection, become aware of various features of my conscious experience ('is it painful?' 'is it clear?'). Kant calls these self-conscious discoveries 'apperceptions'. But there is no such experience as recognizing my consciousness as my own; in Kantian terms this is not an 'empirical apperception', but a 'transcendental apperception'.

Awareness of experiences as my own is at the same time awareness of experiences as belonging to a single consciousness. Here again it is not experience, but the *a priori* activity of the understanding which is at work, making a 'synthesis' of intuitions, combining them into the unity of a single consciousness. This Kant calls 'the transcendental unity of apperception'.

Kant agrees with the empiricist that for any knowledge of objects – even of oneself as an object – experience is necessary. The original unity of apperception gives me only the *concept* of myself; for any *knowledge* of myself, empirical awareness is necessary. But empirical knowledge, whether of myself or of anything else, involves judgement; and there cannot be judgement without concepts. Some concepts are derived from experience, but these depend on others that are presupposed by experience and therefore knowledge even of appearances, knowledge even of myself, must be subject to the categories.

The source of the objective order of nature is the transcendental self: the self that is shown, but not yet known, in the transcendental unity of apperception. The objective nature of the world is derived by Kant from the consciousness of this unity, because it is a unity which is possible only if our experience is experience of a world which is describable by the categories. It is thus that he concludes his transcendental deduction.

7

The system of principles

In the second section of the analytic, the system of principles, Kant sets out a number of *a priori* propositions about experience. Judgements may be analytic or synthetic. The highest principle of analytic judgements is that they must not be self-contradictory: a self-contradictory judgement is void, and the mark of an analytic judgement is that the contradiction of it is self-contradictory. But the principle of non-contradiction will not take us beyond the field of analytic propositions. In the realm of the synthetic it is a necessary but not a sufficient condition for truth.

Kant sets out four principles underpinning synthetic judgements. He calls them (1) axioms of intuition; (2) anticipations of perception; (3) analogies of experience; and (4) postulates of empirical thought. None of these technical terms is illuminating, and some of them are positively misleading. But under each heading he sets out profound and important insights.

The first of these principles is that all experiences have extensive magnitude. Whatever we experience is extended – that is, it has parts distinct from other parts – either in space or in time. In the transcendental aesthetic we were told that any experience must have a place in space and time; now Kant goes further and says that any experience must be spread out in space and time. It is this fact, he maintains, that underpins geometrical axioms, such as the axiom that between two points only one straight line is possible. The claim that every experience has extensive magnitude in space is plausible with regard to vision and touch, but it is not easy to apply to hearing and taste. However, it is reasonable to hold that the experiences of all of the five senses are extended in time.

When, second, Kant speaks of 'anticipations of perception' it sounds as if he is saying that whenever I have an experience, I can predict what experience is coming next. But that is not what he means at all. In all appearances the object of sensation has intensive magnitude. For instance, if you feel a certain degree of heat, you are aware that you could be feeling something hotter or less hot; what you are feeling is a point on a scale which extends in both directions. Similarly, to see a colour is to see something which is located on a spectrum and to hear a sound is to hear something that is pitched upon a scale. Any actual sensation is unpredictable: what is known *a priori* is simply the logical possibility of similar sensations at other points upon a common scale. 'Projection' might be a better word than 'anticipation' to catch Kant's sense.

The third section, headed 'analogies of experience', contains the most far-reaching of Kant's principles. The first analogy states that in all changes of appearances, substance is permanent; the second analogy states that all changes take place in accordance with a law of cause and effect. Each of the two theses takes off from reflection on our awareness of time: time considered first as duration, and then as succession.

Time itself cannot be perceived. We can only be aware of time if we relate atomic momentary phenomena to some permanent substratum. Moreover, if there is to be genuine change, as opposed to mere succession, there has to be something that is first one thing and then another. But this permanent element cannot be supplied by our experience, which is itself in constant flux; it must therefore be supplied by something objective. 'All existence in time and all change in time have to be viewed simply as a mode of the existence of something that remains and persists' (CPR, 301). Thus Kant seeks to establish the necessity of substance.

To establish the necessity of the relation between cause and effect, Kant starts from a simple observation, whose significance he was the first philosopher to see. If I stand still and watch a ship moving down a river I have a succession of different views: first of the ship upstream, then of it downstream, and so on. But equally, if I stand still and look at a house, there will be a certain succession in my experiences: first, perhaps, I look at the roof, then at the upper and lower floors, finally at the basement. What is it that distinguishes between a merely subjective succession of phenomena (the various glimpses of the house) and an objective observation of a change (the motion of the ship downstream)? There is no basis for making the distinction except some necessary causal regularity.

> Let us suppose that there is an event which has nothing preceding it from which it follows according to a rule. All succession in perception would then be only in the apprehension, that is would be merely subjective, and there would be no way to determine which perceptions really came first and which came later. We should then have only a play of impressions relating to no object and it would be impossible in our perceptions to make temporal distinctions between one phenomenon and another.   (CPR, 307–8)

This shows that there is something deeply wrong with Hume's idea that we first perceive temporal succession between events, and then go on to regard one as cause and one as effect. Matters are the other way round: without relationships between cause and effect we cannot establish order in time.

The most important part of the 'postulates of empirical thought' is a brief section headed 'Refutation of idealism'. Kant has in view a twofold target: the problematic idealism of Descartes ('I exist' is the only indubitable empirical assertion), and the dogmatic idealism of Berkeley (the external world is illusory). Common to both of these is the thesis that the inner is better known than the outer, and that outer substances need to be inferred from inner experiences.

Kant's argument against these assumptions goes as follows. I am aware of changing mental states, and thus I am conscious of my existence in time: that is, as having experiences first at one time and then at another. But, as has just been argued, the perception of change involves the perception of something permanent. But this something permanent is not myself; the unifying subject of my experience is not itself an object of experience. Hence, only if I have outer experience is it possible for me to make judgements about the past.

Kant's analytic closes with an insistence on the limits of the competence of the intellect. The categories cannot determine their own applicability, the principles cannot establish their own truth. Intellect alone cannot establish that there is any such thing as a substance, or that every change has a cause. All that can be established *a priori*, whether by the transcendental deduction of the categories or by the exposition of the system of the principles, is that *if experience is to be possible* certain conditions must hold.

Kant observes that philosophers make a distinction between phenomena (appearances) and noumena (objects of thought), and divide the world into a world of the senses and a world of the intellect. His own analytic has shown that there cannot be a world of mere appearances, mere objects of sense which do not fall under any categories or instantiate any rules. But we cannot conclude from this that there is a non-sensible world which is discovered by the intellect alone. The domain of the intellect, Kant concludes, is an island:

> It is the land of truth – enchanting name – surrounded by a wide and stormy ocean, the native home of illusion, where many a fog bank and many a swiftly melting iceberg give the deceptive appearance of farther shores, deluding the adventurous seafarer ever new with empty hopes.
>
> (CPR, 339)

To accept the existence of noumena as extra-sensible objects which can be studied by the use of intellect alone is to enter into this realm of illusion. In his transcendental dialectic Kant takes us on an exploratory tour of this world of enchantment.

8

The transcendental dialectic

In the critical venture of his transcendental dialectic Kant has three principal targets: metaphysical psychology, metaphysical cosmology and metaphysical theology. 'Pure reason', he tells us, 'furnished the idea for a transcendental doctrine of the soul, for a transcendental science of the world, and finally for a transcendental knowledge of God.' In turn he tests to destruction the corresponding three notions of an immaterial immortal soul, of a surveyable cosmic whole, and of an absolutely necessary being.

The critique of metaphysical psychology is entitled 'The Paralogisms of Pure Reason' – 'paralogism' being his term for a fallacious argument. The section is a sustained attack on the Cartesian view of mind. Kant begins by agreeing with Descartes that the thought 'I am thinking' must accompany every other possible thought. Self-consciousness is inseparable from thought, because self-consciousness is necessary if we are to have the thought of thinking. He goes on, however, to disagree sharply with the conclusions that Descartes drew from his *Cogito*.

Rational psychology, Kant says, 'professes to be a science built upon the single proposition *I am thinking*'. It purports to be a study of an unknown X, the transcendental subject of thinking, 'the I or he or it (the thing) that is thinking' (CPR, 412–14). An empirical psychology would limit itself to the study of the deliverances of the inner senses, but our

33

natural drive to go beyond the limits of merely empirical psychology leads us into fallacies.

Kant lists four such paralogisms, which can be crudely summarized as follows: (1) from 'Necessarily the thinking subject is a subject' we conclude 'The thinking subject is a necessary subject'; (2) from 'Dividing up the ego makes no sense' we conclude 'The ego is an indivisible substance'; (3) from 'Whenever I am conscious, it is the same I who am conscious' we conclude 'Whenever I am conscious, I am conscious of the same I'; (4) from 'I can think of myself without my body' we conclude 'Without my body I can think of myself'. On the basis of these paralogisms, rational psychology concludes that the self is an immaterial, incorruptible, personal, immortal entity. The proof, Kant says, has never really exercised any influence upon the common reason of men. 'It so stands upon the point of a hair, that even the schools preserve it from falling only so long as they keep it unceasingly spinning round like a top' (CPR, 454).

Kant's attack on *a priori* cosmology is delivered in a set of antinomies. An antinomy is a pair of contrasting arguments that lead to contradictory conclusions – a thesis and an antithesis. The thesis of the first antinomy is 'The world had a beginning in time' and the antithesis is 'The world had no beginning in time'.

Kant proposes that both statements can be proved: not, of course, to show that there are two contradictory truths, but to show instead the impotence of reason to talk about 'the world' as a whole (CPR, 471–5). The argument for the thesis is this: An infinite series is one that can never be completed, and so it cannot be the case that an infinite series of temporal states has already passed away. The argument for the antithesis is this: If the world had a beginning, then there was a time when the world did not exist. There is nothing to differentiate any moment of this 'void time' from any other; hence there can be no answer to the question 'Why did the world begin when it did?'

The second antinomy concentrates not on time but on space – or rather, on the spatial divisibility of substances. The thesis is 'Every composite substance in the world is made up of simple parts'; the antithesis 'No composite thing in the world is made up of simple parts'. The thesis is the affirmation, and the antithesis the denial, of atomism.

The third antinomy differs from the previous two. In the first two antinomies both the thesis and the antithesis were rejected as false. But when Kant comes to the third antinomy he seeks to show that, properly interpreted, both thesis and antithesis are true. The thesis argues that natural causality is not sufficient to explain the phenomena of the world; in addition to determining causes we must take account of freedom and spontaneity. The antithesis argues that to postulate transcendental freedom is to resign oneself to blind lawlessness, since the intrusion of an undetermined cause would disrupt the whole explanatory system of nature.

Kant seeks to show that freedom properly understood is compatible with determinism properly understood. An event may be both determined by nature and grounded in freedom. The human will, he claims, is sensuous but free: that is to say, it is affected by passion but it is not necessitated by passion. Humans have a power of self-determination, but the exercise of this power has two aspects, sensory (perceptible in experience) and intelligible (graspable only by the intellect). Our free agency is the intelligible cause of sensible effects; and these sensible phenomena are also part of an unbroken series in accordance with unchangeable laws. To reconcile human freedom with deterministic nature, Kant claims that nature operates in time, whereas the human will, as noumenon rather than phenomenon, as object of thought rather than object of appearance, is outside time.

Kant's fourth antinomy concerns necessity and contingency. The thesis is that the series of contingent beings ends with a necessary being, and the antithesis is that the series goes on for ever. The details of his argument will be considered when we turn to metaphysical theology, but we can now stop to note the way in which the antinomies resemble each other. In each of the antinomies, the antithesis affirms that a certain series continues for ever, the thesis that the same series comes to a full stop. Thus:

> First: the series of items *next to* each other in space and in time comes to an end (thesis)/goes on for ever (antithesis)

> Second: the series of items which are *parts of* others comes to an end (thesis)/goes on for ever (antithesis)

> Third: the series of items *caused by* another ends in a free, naturally uncaused, event (thesis)/goes on for ever (antithesis)

> Fourth: the series of items *contingent upon* another ends with an absolutely necessary being (thesis)/goes on for ever (antithesis)

Each of the italicized relationships is regarded by Kant as a form of *being conditioned* by something else: so that each of these series is a series of conditions, and in each argument the thesis concludes with an unconditioned absolute.

According to Kant both sides of each antinomy, except the third, are in error: the thesis is the error of dogmatism, the antithesis the error of empiricism. The thesis always represents the world as smaller than thought: we can think beyond it. The antithesis always represents the world as larger than thought: we cannot think to the end of it. 'In all cases the cosmical idea is either too large or too small for the empirical regress.' We must match thought and the world by trimming our cosmic idea to fit the empirical inquiry.

Kant's attack on his final target, metaphysical theology, is based on the pre-critical treatment of the subject in his *Only Possible Argument*. There he divided arguments for God's existence into two classes: ontological and cosmological. Now he lists three classes of arguments, subdividing the second class into those which derive from the general nature of the empirical world, which he continues to call cosmological, and physico-theological proofs, which start from particular natural phenomena.

As in his earlier work, Kant argues against the ontological argument for the existence of necessary being on the grounds that in its standard use 'is' is not a predicate, but a copula, a simple link between predicate and subject. If, however, we say 'God is' or 'There is a God', Kant says, 'we attach no new predicate to the concept of God, but only posit the subject in itself with all its predicates'. A concept has to be determinate prior to being compared to reality, otherwise we would not know *which* concept was being compared and found to correspond, or not correspond, to reality. *That* there is a God cannot be part of what we mean by 'God'; hence 'There is a God' cannot be an analytic proposition, and the ontological argument must fail.

Kant was wrong to think that the failure of the onto-logical argument implied that all arguments for the exist-ence of God collapsed. What his criticism does show is that there is an incoherence in the notion of a being whose essence implies its existence. But a cosmological argument need not purport to show the existence of such a being, but only of one which is uncaused, unchanging and everlasting, in contrast to the caused, variable and contingent items in the world of experience.

Kant in fact has a criticism of the cosmological argument which is independent of his rebuttal of the ontological argument. All forms of the cosmological argument seek to show that a series of contingent causes, however long, can be completed only by a necessary cause. But we are faced with a dilemma if we ask whether the necessary cause is, or is not, part of the chain of causes. If it is part of the chain, then we can raise in its case, as in the case of the other mem-bers of the chain, the question why it exists. But we cannot imagine a supreme being saying to itself 'I am from eter-nity to eternity, and outside me there is nothing save what is through my will, *but whence then am I?*' On the other hand, if the necessary being is not part of the chain of causation, how can it be its first member and account for all the other links which end with the existence of the likes of us?

The argument for God's existence which is most gently treated by Kant is the physico-theological proof. It must always, he says, be mentioned with respect. His aim, here as earlier, is not to diminish its authority, but to limit the scope of its conclusion. The proof argues that everywhere in the world we find signs of order, in accordance with a determinate purpose, carried out with great wisdom. This order is alien to the individual things in the world which contribute to make it up; it must therefore have been imposed by one or more sublime wise causes, operating not blindly as nature does, but freely as humans do. Kant raises various difficulties about the analogies which this argument draws between the operation of nature and the artifice of human skill. But even if we waive these, the most the argument can prove is the existence of 'an *architect* of the world who is always very much hampered by the adaptability of the material in which he works, not a *creator* of the world to whose idea everything is subject'.

9

The *Groundwork of the Metaphysics of Morals*

In the 1780s Kant published two books which he saw as in different ways supplementary to the *Critique of Pure Reason.* Early reviewers of that book criticized it as being too close to the empiricism of Berkeley and Hume. Kant felt he had been misunderstood and in 1783 published *Prolegomena to Any Future Metaphysic,* which he regarded as a shorter and simpler version of the *Critique.* And just as the first *Critique* set out critically the synthetic *a priori* principles of theoretical reason, the *Groundwork of the Metaphysics of Morals* (1785) set out critically the synthetic *a priori* principles of practical reason.

The starting point of Kant's moral system is that the only thing which is good without qualification is a good will. Talents, character, self-control and fortune can be used to bad ends as well as good. The goodness of a good will is not to be judged on the basis of what it achieves; good will is good in itself alone:

> Even if, by some special disfavour of destiny, or by the niggardly endowment of stepmotherly nature, this will is entirely lacking in power to carry out its intentions; if by its utmost effort it still accomplishes nothing, and only good will is left . . . even then it would still shine like a jewel for its own sake as something which has its full value in itself.
>
> (GM, 394)

Earlier moralists had taught that happiness was the ultimate purpose of morality, but Kant argues that even happiness can be corrupting. It was not in order to pursue happiness that human beings were endowed with a will; instinct would have been far more effective for this purpose. Reason was given to us in order to produce a will which was good not as a means to some further end, but good in itself.

According to Kant a will is good only if it is motivated by duty. What is it, then, to act out of duty? A first answer is to say that it is to act as the moral law prescribes. But acting in accordance with duty is not the same as acting from the motive of duty. A grocer who chooses honesty as the best policy, or a philanthropist who takes delight in pleasing others, may perform actions that are in accord with duty. Such actions conform to the moral law, but they are not motivated by reverence for it. Actions of this kind, however correct and amiable, have, according to Kant, no moral worth. Worth of character is shown only when someone does good not from inclination but from duty. A man who is wholly wretched and longs to die, but preserves his own life solely out of a sense of duty – that is Kant's paradigm of good willing (GM, 398).

The way to test whether one is acting out of a sense of duty is to seek the maxim, or principle, on which one acts, that is to say, the imperative to which one's act conforms. There are two sorts of imperative: hypothetical and categorical. A hypothetical imperative says: If you wish to achieve a certain end, act in such-and-such a way. The categorical imperative says: No matter what end you wish to achieve, act in such-and-such a way. There are many hypothetical imperatives, because there are many different ends which humans may set themselves. There is only one categorical imperative, which is: 'Act only according to a maxim by which you can at the same time will that it shall become a universal law.'

Kant illustrates the operation of the categorical imperative with a number of examples, of which we may mention two. The first is this. Having run out of funds, I may be tempted to borrow money, though I know that I will be unable to repay it:

> I have then to ask myself 'Should I really be content that my maxim (the maxim of getting out of a difficulty by a false promise) should hold as a universal law (one valid both for myself and others)? And could I really say to myself that every one may make a false promise if he finds himself in a difficulty from which he can extricate himself in no other way?' I then become aware at once that I can indeed will to lie, but I can by no means will a universal law of lying; for by such a law there could properly be no promises at all.
>
> (GM, 57)

A second example is this. A person who is well provided for, and is asked for help by others suffering hardship, may be tempted to respond, 'What does this matter to me? Let every one be as happy as Heaven wills or as he can make himself; I won't harm him, but I won't help him either.' He cannot will this maxim to be universalized, because a situation might arise in which he himself needed love and sympathy from others.

These cases illustrate two different ways in which the categorical imperative applies. In the first case, the maxim cannot be universalized because its universalization involves contradiction (if no one keeps promises, there is no such thing as promising). In the second case, the maxim can be universalized without contradiction, but no one could rationally *will* the situation which would result from its universalization. Kant says the two different cases correspond to two different kinds of duty: strict duties (such as that of not lying), and meritorious duties (such as that of helping the needy).

Not all Kant's examples are convincing. He argues, for instance, that the categorical imperative excludes suicide. But however wrong suicide may be, there is nothing self-contradictory in the prospect of universal suicide; and someone disgusted with the human race might well applaud the prospect. However, Kant has a further formulation of the categorical imperative that may be more effective in ruling out suicide. It runs 'Act in such a way that you always treat humanity, whether in your own person or in the person of any other, never simply as a means, but always at the same time as an end.' To take one's own life, Kant urges, is to use one's own person as a means of bringing to an end one's discomfort and distress. But it is hard to see just what else this rule excludes, since we all every day make use of others – whether plumbers or lawyers – as means to our own ends. We need to be told more about what it is to treat people 'at the same time as an end'.

As a human being, Kant says, I am not only an end in myself, I am a member of a kingdom of ends, a union of rational beings under common laws. My will, as has been said, is rational in so far as its maxims can be made universal laws. The converse of this is that universal law is law which is made by rational wills like mine. A rational being 'is subject only to laws which are made by himself and yet are universal'. In the kingdom of ends, we are all both legislators and subjects.

In the kingdom of ends, everything has a price or a worth. If something has a price, it can be exchanged for something else. What has worth is unique and unexchangeable; it is beyond price. There are, Kant says, two kinds of price: market price, which is related to the satisfaction of need; and fancy price, which is related to the satisfaction of taste.

Morality is above and beyond either kind of price: it is the only thing which has worth. Skill and diligence in work have a market price; wit, lively imagination and humour have a fancy price; but fidelity to promises and kindness based on principle (not on instinct) have an intrinsic worth.

10

The *Critique of Practical Reason*

Three years after the *Groundwork* appeared Kant returned to the topic of ethics with a *Critique of Practical Reason* (1788). Here he sought to relate his moral theory to the account he had given of the human mind in his first *Critique*. The categorical imperative, like the principles of the analytic, is a synthetic *a priori* judgement, but unlike them it is addressed not to the understanding but to the will.

In humans, Kant tells us, there is a lower faculty of desire and a higher faculty of the will. The faculty of desire aims at achieving pleasure and avoiding displeasure; the imperatives that determine it are all hypothetical imperatives, and vary from person to person. The will on the other hand obeys the categorical imperative and the laws of which it is itself a legislator. The will therefore is autonomous, that is, self regulating, whereas desires, determined by external and internal causes, are heteronomous, regulated by others.

A moral imperative seems so different from a statement of physics that it seems at first odd to think that it can, like such a statement, be categorized as analytic or synthetic, *a priori* or *a posteriori*. The link between the two is made by the notion of law. Kant tells us in the second *Critique*:

> Nature in the most general sense is the existence of things under laws. The sensory nature of rational beings in general

is their existence under empirically conditioned laws and is
thus, for that reason, heteronomy. The supersensory nature
of the same beings, on the other hand, is their existence in
accordance with laws that are independent of any empirical
condition and thus belong to the autonomy of pure reason ...
The law of this autonomy is the moral law, which is therefore
the fundamental law of a supersensible nature, and of a pure
world of the intellect, the counterpart of which is to exist
in the sensible world but without infringing upon its laws.

(GM, 174)

The autonomous will, Kant tells us, is the sole principle of
all moral laws and of the corresponding duties. Particular
laws and particular duties are the matter of the objects
of the will, but what makes the individual's maxims into
practical laws is something formal rather than material. It
is the fact that they are fit for a giving of universal law.
This lawgiving form is the only thing that can constitute a
determining ground of the will.

If the will is to be autonomous, it must be free from being
determined by any necessary causation. But how can that
be? Kant himself tells us that if it were possible for us to
know someone's mind and its incentives, we could calculate
her conduct for the future with as much certainty as a lunar
or solar eclipse. Nevertheless, he tells us, it is still possible
to maintain that a human being's conduct is free. He would
never have ventured to introduce freedom into science, he
admits, had not the moral law, and with it practical reason,
come in and forced this concept on us.

The concept is forced on us in the following way. The
moral law teaches us that we are obliged to do certain
things. But 'ought' implies 'can'. Therefore we must have
it in our power to do those things. Kant believes that this

logical deduction can be supported by experience, or at least by a thought experiment. If you are threatened with execution unless you carry out an immoral command, you do not know what you would do. But, Kant says, you must admit without hesitation that it would be possible for you to refrain from the wicked deed. Therefore you acknowledge a freedom within you which without the moral law you would not have known.

Kant rises to heights of rhetoric as he surveys the derivation of freedom from duty:

> Duty! Sublime and mighty name ... what origin is worthy of you? ... It is nothing other than personality, that is freedom and independence from the mechanism of the whole of nature. (GM, 210)

The practical freedom that is required for duty can be defined as the independence of the will from anything other than the moral law alone (GM, 215).

To reconcile the concept of causality as freedom with the concept of causality as natural necessity, we have to distinguish between the phenomenal world of appearances and the noumenal world of things in themselves. Appearances take place in a time series, but things in themselves are outside time. A human agent in every action is both free and subject to necessity. While aware of herself as subject to the mechanism of nature, she is also conscious of herself as a thing in itself and free from time conditions. As the latter, she is determined only by self-imposed laws and is therefore free.

It is difficult to reconcile this with the fact that our free actions have effects at particular times in the sensible world. We will consider later whether, despite this, it is possible to rescue Kant's claim that human freedom is compatible with physical determinism.

The climax of Kant's second *Critique* comes when he considers what is the highest good. The highest good, by definition, is the necessary highest end of a morally determined will. The highest good in an individual, he tells us, is constituted by virtue plus happiness. The highest good in an entire world consists in happiness distributed in accord with morality. If the achievement of the highest good is to be possible three preconditions are necessary, which Kant calls postulates of practical reasoning. These are God, freedom and immortality.

Freedom we have already considered at length. The postulate of the existence of God is presented in a manner that shows that the concept of God belongs in origin, as Kant says, not to physics but to morals. The argument goes thus. It is a duty for us to promote the highest good. But the highest good is possible only under the condition of the existence of God; hence it is morally necesssary to assume the existence of God. God's aim in creating the world was not human happiness. It was, rather, the highest good – which adds a condition, namely that humans should be worthy of happiness.

The postulate of immortality is argued for thus. Complete conformity of the will with the moral law is holiness, a perfection of which no rational being of the sensible world is capable at any stage of his existence. Since it is nevertheless required as practically necessary, it can only be found in an endless progress towards that complete conformity. Such endless progress is possible only on the presupposition of the existence and personality of the same rational being continuing endlessly, and that is what is meant by the immortality of the soul.

By these three postulates Kant restores to the reader the three great objects of metaphysics, God, freedom and immortality, which he had exposed as illusions in the first *Critique*. Does this mean that what was shown as transcendent for speculative reason now appears immanent for practical reason? Certainly, says Kant, but only for practical purposes. In accepting these postulates we know nothing of the real nature of our souls, nor the intelligible world, nor the supreme being.

Kant concludes the main part of the second *Critique* with the famous lines that sum up the whole of his philosophy: 'Two things fill the mind with ever new and increasing admiration and reverence, the more often and more steadily one reflects on them: the starry heavens above me and the moral law within me' (GM, 269).

11

The analytic of the beautiful

Kant's analytic of the beautiful, in his *Critique of the Power of Judgment* (1788), takes its start from the notion of taste. He is not however concerned with the sensation of taste, as occurring, for example, when one tastes a particular wine. Such tastes strike different people differently, and they do not lead to disputes. I prefer Chardonnay to Sauvignon Blanc, but I have no quarrel with those who have the opposite preference. Such differences, in Kant's terminology, are differences about what is or is not *agreeable*. Animals, no less than humans, can find things agreeable or disagreeable.

When Kant speaks of the judgement of taste he means something rather grander: a judgement that something is beautiful. Such a judgement is not a matter of logic or knowledge, but is based on the feeling of pleasure or displeasure in an object. It is not the same as a judgement of goodness. If I am to judge an object good I must always know what sort of thing it is supposed to be. If I want to know whether an X is a good X, I need to know what Xs are for – that is how I tell what makes a good knife, or a good plumber, and so on. I do not need anything similar in order to find beauty in something. This is shown, for instance, by abstract art.

The judgement of taste – unlike a judgement that something is agreeable – is disinterested. 'Taste', Kant says, 'is the faculty of judging of an object or a method of representing it by an *entirely disinterested* satisfaction or dissatisfaction' (GM, 96). One is not appreciating the sheer beauty of a Titian nude if one is sexually excited by it. The taste for beauty, unlike the appreciation of goodness, is completely disinterested, because the practical reason that determines goodness has reference to our own well-being. To point out the difference, Kant remarks that while we can distinguish between what is good in itself and what is good only as a means, we do not make any parallel distinction between what is beautiful as a means and what is beautiful as an end.

All judgements of taste are singular, but they claim a universal validity. If I think that a poem, a building or a symphony is beautiful, I impute to others an obligation to agree with me. Judgements of taste are singular in form ('this rose is beautiful') but universal in import; they are, as Kant puts it, expressions of 'a universal voice'. Yet, because a judgement of taste does not bring its object under a concept, no reason can be given for it, and no argument can constrain agreement to it. To convince another of the beauty of an object you have to bring it before his eyes.

How can it be legitimate to make a singular judgement that claims universal validity? A judgement of taste is a kind of synthetic judgement in which the place of a predicate is taken by a satisfaction that accompanies the perception of the object. It is, however, *a priori* in so far as it concerns the assent of others. It is an empirical judgement that I perceive and judge an object with pleasure. When I make such a judgement, I do not claim that everyone will agree with me, but I do claim that everyone ought to do so. So it is an *a priori* judgement that I find it beautiful, that I demand the satisfaction of everyone else.

We have here another instance of the recurrent problem of the deduction of the synthetic *a priori*. Kant's answer to the problem goes like this. A judgement of beauty, not based on reason, can claim universal validity only if we are all in possession of a common sensibility (*Gemeinsinn*) – a sensibility which, since it is normative, cannot derive from experience but must be transcendental.

For Kant there are two kinds of beauty: free beauty (*pulchritudo vaga*) and derivative beauty (*pulchritudo adhaerens*). The first presupposes no concept of what the object ought to be; the second does presuppose such a concept, and the perfection of the object in accordance therewith. The first is called the self-subsistent beauty of this or that thing; the second, as dependent upon a concept (conditioned beauty), is ascribed to objects with a particular purpose. A judgement of beauty without reference to any purpose that an object is to serve is a pure judgement of taste. Kant's regular paradigm of a free natural beauty is a simple flower. As for the other kind of beauty:

> Human beauty (i.e. of a man, a woman, or a child), the beauty of a horse, or a building (be it church, palace, arsenal or summer house), presupposes a concept of the purpose which determines what the thing is to be, and consequently a concept of its perfection; it is therefore derivative beauty.
>
> (GM, 100–1)

It is clear from this passage that Kant's aesthetic is much more at home with natural beauty than with the beauty of artefacts.

Kant adjoins to his analytic of beauty an 'analytic of the sublime'. He begins with a distinction between two kinds of sublimity, which he calls (not very happily) the mathematical and the dynamical. In each case the sublime object is vast, great, overwhelming; but in the mathematical case what is overwhelmed is our perception, and in the dynamical case what is overwhelmed is our power. Whatever is mathematically sublime is too great to be taken in by any of our senses; it awakens in us the feeling of a faculty above sense which reaches out towards infinity. Whatever is dynamically sublime is something to which any resistance on our part would be vain, but which yet allows us to remain without fear in a state of security.

> Bold, overhanging, and as it were threatening rocks; clouds piled up in the sky, moving with lightning flashes and thunder peals; volcanoes in all their violence of destruction; hurricanes with their track of devastation; the boundless ocean in a state of tumult; the lofty waterfall of a mighty river, and such like – these exhibit our faculty of resistance as insignificantly small in comparison with their might. But the sight of them is the more attractive, the more fearful it is, provided only that we are in security; and we willingly call these objects sublime, because they raise the energies of the soul above their accustomed height and discover in us a faculty of resistance of a quite different kind, which gives us courage to measure ourselves against the apparent almightiness of nature.   (GM, 144–5)

We cannot count on universal assent to judgements of the sublime as we can to judgements of beauty. 'What we, prepared by culture, call sublime, will appear merely repellent to the unrefined person.' We have no right to complain if a Savoyard peasant thinks that the devotees of the icy mountains are no better than idiots.

Nature can be both beautiful and sublime, but art can only be beautiful. Kant believed that the beautiful in nature is pre-eminent over beauty in art because appreciation of art is compatible with wickedness. But to take an immediate interest in the beauty of nature, he maintained, is always the mark of a good soul. What then is the relation between the two kinds of beauty? Kant's answer is subtle. On the one hand, nature is beautiful because it looks like art. On the other hand, if we are to admire a beautiful work of art, we must be conscious that it is artificial and not natural; yet 'the purposiveness in its form must seem to be as free from constraint by rule just as if it were a product of mere nature' (GM, 185). For the judgement of beautiful art taste is needed; for the production of such art what is needed is genius.

The production of beauty is the purpose of art, but artificial beauty is not a thing that is beautiful, but a beautiful representation of a thing. Beautiful art can indeed present as beautiful things that in nature are ugly or repellent. There are three kinds of beautiful arts, each with their beautiful products. First, there are the arts of speech, namely rhetoric and poetry. Then there are what Kant calls the formative arts, namely painting and the plastic arts of sculpture and architecture. Finally, there is a third class of art which creates a play of sensations: the most important of these is music. 'Of all the arts,' says Kant, '*poetry* (which owes its origin almost entirely to genius and will least be guided by precept or example) maintains the first rank' (GM, 170).

Kant attaches to his treatment of the beautiful and the sublime an appendix on the comic. Wittgenstein once said that there could be a work of philosophy consisting of nothing but jokes, and Aristotle no doubt treated of jokes in his lost work on comedy. But Kant is unusual among great philosophers in offering a serious treatment of humour and laughter.

Admittedly, the jokes he offers as specimens are not very good jokes. He tells the story of a merchant bringing home his fortune from India who was forced to throw all his merchandise overboard in a terrible storm. This upset him so much that his wig turned grey overnight. If well told, Kant assures us, this story will move a dinner table to peals of laughter. On its basis he offers a theory of the comic. A joke must contain something that deceives for a short period. Once the illusion is removed the mind bounces back like a ball hit by a racket. There is a corresponding bodily movement, 'a tensing and relaxing of the elastic parts of our viscera which communicates itself to our diaphragm'. This is laughter, which is something extremely conducive to health. Voltaire once said that heaven has given us two comforts against the burdens of life, namely hope and sleep. Kant tells us that he should have added a third: laughter.

12

Teleology in nature

Having completed his analysis of the aesthetic power of judgement Kant offers, in the second part of his treatise on the power of judgement, a 'critique of the teleological power of judgement'. As a first approximation, what he means by this power is the ability to detect purposiveness in nature.

Natural objects stand to each other in relations of cause and effect. But they also serve one another as means and ends. Philosophers have called the first relationship efficient or mechanical causality, and the second relationship final causality (or, equivalently, teleological causality). Kant maintains that nature cannot be adequately understood without both kinds of causality. If we are to explain, for instance, the structure of a bird, the hollowness of its bones, the placement of its wings for movement and of its tail for steering, and so on, we will find that mere mechanical causality is enough without introducing final causality. But this, he says, is not adequate for the idea of nature as the sum of empirical objects.

To avoid misunderstanding we must distinguish at the outset between internal purposiveness and relative purposiveness. River deposits encourage the growth of vegetables that are useful for humans; but this is not to be judged as an internal end of nature. Even if humans find things in nature advantageous (e.g. feathers for clothing and horses for riding) one cannot assume here even a relative end of nature – unless the existence of humans is itself an end of nature. A thing exists as a natural end if it is cause and effect of itself: for example, a tree generates another tree, but also generates itself as an individual. Leaves are products of a tree, yet they in turn operate for its welfare.

A natural product that is also a natural end must be related to itself reciprocally as both cause and effect. Besides mechanical causation,

> a causal nexus can also be observed in accordance with a concept of reason (of ends) which, if considered as a series, would carry with it descending as well as ascending dependency, in which the thing which is on the one hand designated as an effect nevertheless deserves in ascent, the name of a cause of the same thing of which it is an effect. (GM, 244)

The parts of a natural whole are reciprocally the cause and effect of their form.

Teleological causality has objective reality, but cannot be drawn from experience. We are led, Kant says, to a concept of nature as a system in accordance with the rule of ends. He is not, however, presenting nature as a system of intelligent design. The scientific study of the purposiveness of nature should be carried out in abstraction from the question whether the ends of nature are or are not the subject of anyone's intention. We cannot infer the existence of an intelligent designer. It is simply that humans like us cannot conceive of the possibility of a teleological world except by conceiving an intentionally acting supreme cause. But the concept of God should not be brought into natural science.

Kant presents not only an analytic but a dialectic of the teleological power, including an antinomy in parallel with the ones presented in the first *Critique*. The thesis of the antinomy is that all production of things in nature takes place in accordance with strictly mechanical laws. The antithesis is that some production of things in nature is not possible in accordance with strictly mechanical laws.

If the thesis and antithesis are taken as statements of fact, they do indeed contradict each other and neither of them can be proved. But they should in fact be taken as maxims for research. In accordance with the thesis, a scientist should never cease to look for explanation in terms of mechanical causes. But in accordance with the antithesis, he must realize that we will never be able to make sense of the structures and activities of organic beings without attending to their teleological purposes.

However ubiquitous teleology may be, when we go through the whole of creation we do not find in it, as nature, anything that can claim to be its final end. Why do plants exist? Why do herbivores exist? If we think of human beings as objects in nature, we can ask the same question about them too. It is hard to give an answer, since collectively they work so hard for the destruction of their own species. The only ultimate end Kant can think of for humans is culture, culture pursued in a cosmopolitan community. Only of the human being as a moral being can it be seriously asked for what purpose it exists. A good will is that alone by means of which man's existence can have an absolute value. Only in relation to that can the existence of the world have a final end.

The last section of the third *Critique* repeats what Kant has already said more than once about the limits of the physico-theological proof. 'For the human reason any theoretical proof of the original being as a divinity or of the soul as an immortal spirit is absolutely impossible.' Any object that we have to conceive *a priori* to make possible the use of pure practical reason in obedience to duty cannot be anything more than a matter of faith.

The two treatises that make up the third *Critique* – that on aesthetics and that on teleology – look at first as if they are concerned with two quite distinct subject matters. However, Kant appended an introduction in which he explains that they belong to a single venture because they deal with a single power, the power of judgement. This power provides an intermediary between the theoretical intellect, which legislates for the realm of nature, and the practical reason, which legislates for the realm of freedom.

There are, according to Kant, three fundamental human capacities: that for knowing, that for feeling pleasure and pain, and that for willing. The power of judgement is placed between the intellect and the practical reason in the same way as the feeling of pleasure belongs between the faculty for knowing and the faculty for willing.

Kant's discussion of the two activities of the power of judgement brings out the importance of aesthetic factors in science. A number of principles of research are not empirical discoveries but rather aesthetic guidelines, such as the quest for simplicity, and the search for the least possible number of explanatory factors. The very notion of viewing nature as a single whole is an aesthetic rather than an empirical ideal. The discovery that heterogeneous scientific laws can be unified into a single system, Kant tells us, is for the scientist 'the ground of a very noticeable pleasure'.

13

Religion within the Boundaries of Mere Reason

At the end of the preface to the *Critique of the Power of Judgment* Kant tells us that this work brings his entire critical enterprise to an end. But he continued to write and his next major publication was *Religion within the Boundaries of Mere Reason* in 1792. He offered the book as an essay in theology: not the biblical theology of the Scripture scholar, but a purely philosophical theology.

Morality in itself, he begins, has no need for religion, either as a motive or an aid. It is contemptible to need a further end in responding to the demands of duty. However, 'ought' implies 'can': obligation entails ability. But mere humans are not capable of adequate response; and hence arises the idea of a mighty moral lawgiver. In that way, morality inevitably leads to religion (WG, 59). But there is a difference between natural and revealed religion. In natural religion I know something is a divine command because I know it is a duty; in revealed religion I know it is a duty because it is a divine command.

Whereas in his earlier treatments of theology, in *The Only Possible Argument* and the *Critique of Practical Reason*, Kant seemed anxious to use philosophy to support religion, in this work he seems more concerned to use reason to curb the pretensions of Christianity and to purge its doctrines of irrational elements.

Consider first the doctrine of the fall of man and original sin. Human beings, Kant says, have bad dispositions as well as good ones. At the level of animality there are vices such as lust and gluttony; at the level of humanity there are vices such as jealousy and rivalry. At the level of personality there is a propensity for moral evil: we may fail to comply with good maxims, or comply with them through mixed motives, or adopt positively evil maxims. We have only to look around to see that humans have a propensity for evil.

What is the origin of this propensity for evil? The most inappropriate answer, Kant tells us, is to imagine it as being inherited from our first parents; if that were so it would not be imputable to later generations. Evil, as Kant interprets the Bible, begins not with a propensity, but with a single sinful deed. A man has to make himself into good or evil. A human becomes good only in incessant labouring and becoming (WG, 92).

Consider next the doctrine of the Incarnation of God in Jesus Christ. It is a universal human duty to elevate ourselves to an ideal of moral perfection; this is practical faith in the Son of God. This ideal is one we ought to conform to, and therefore we must be able to do so. The idea of a human being who is morally pleasing to God is present already in our reason. To accept Jesus as a model we need only see in him a course of life entirely blameless; we do not need to accept the accounts of his miracles as well. In practical affairs we cannot count on miracles or take them into consideration in the employment of our reason.

Can we make sense of the notion that Jesus made vicarious satisfaction for our sins? Well, Kant tells us, every human being must die to his old self and put on a new being. The suffering which the new human being must endure, while dying to the old, is depicted in the story of a representative of humankind suffering death once and for all (WG, 115). What are we to make of the notion of Jesus' virgin birth? This doctrine represents a child untainted by moral blemish as one whose seed was not present in a sinful progenitor. Kant observes that this explanation will not do unless we assume that seeds pre-exist only on the male side. 'But what is the use of all this theorizing pro or contra when it suffices for practical purposes to hold the idea itself before us as model?' (WG, 119)

Finally, what of the resurrection of Christ and his ascension into heaven? Kant says that this story 'cannot be used in the interest of religion within the boundaries of pure reason, whatever its historical standing' (WG, 157). The reason is that it implies a materialistic account of human identity. We should prefer, he says, 'the spiritualist hypothesis that a body can remain dead on earth and the same person still be living'.

So much, then, for the life of Christ. What are we to say about the Christian Church? Because a human being, as soon as he is among others, is assailed by vice, it is necessary to set up a society in accordance with the laws of virtue. The ideal of such a state, Kant tells us, has an objective reality in human reason, in the duty to join such a state. An ethical community, unlike a political state, comprises the totality of humankind. Each of us has a duty to become a member of an ethical community. The public lawgiver of such a community must be someone other than the people and so an ethical community is conceivable as a people under divine commands, that is as a people of God.

How could one hope, Kant asks, to construct something so straight from the crooked timber of humanity? We can only wish that God's kingdom will come, and in preparation for it construct a church. A true church must be universal, without sects; pure (without superstition or enthusiasm); free (without hierarchy or illuminism); unchangeable in fundamental constitution. This, he tells us, is what the Creed means when it calls the Church one, holy, catholic and apostolic (WG, 136).

If we consider humans simply as humans, no laws are needed other than the divine moral laws that individuals can recognize in their own conscience. But if we consider them as citizens of a divine state, we need a church with contingent and manifold laws, for which a revelation is necessary. In the moulding of men into an ethical community, church-faith precedes pure religious faith, and for this a holy scripture is needful.

There can be only one true religion, but there can be many faiths: 'The so-called religious struggles . . . have never been anything but squabbles over ecclesiastical faiths.' Empirical faiths have been dealt to us by chance: we need to interpret their scriptures, if at all possible, in accordance with pure religion. This may lead us to forced interpretations of certain texts, such as the psalms that pray for revenge. In the end, Kant hopes, religion will gradually be freed from all regulations that rest on history and all provisional communities of believers. Privately, he believes, we all feel an uncertainty about which among the historical faiths is the right one. This does not matter, however, because moral faith is everywhere the same (WG, 160).

In the religion of reason there is no need for officials, since the members get their orders directly from the legislator. A church, on the other hand, needs an administration and a congregation. A religion can be both natural and revealed, and indeed the Christian religion is both at the same time. Christ was not the founder of religion, but of the first true Church. Kant offers his own version of the great commandment to love God above all and one's neighbour as oneself. It runs thus: 'Do your duty from no other incentive except the unmediated appreciation of duty itself, and promote everyone's welfare from a goodwill not derived from selfish incentives' (WG, 182).

Kant concludes by distinguishing between religion, enthusiasm and superstition. Two forms of delusion lay traps for the religious believer. The delusion that we can distinguish the effects of grace from those of virtue is enthusiasm; the delusion that through acts of cult we can justify ourselves before God is superstition. Enthusiasm, according to Kant, is worse than superstition. But superstition lays the basis for priestcraft, which arises when a church places its essence in observances rather than moral principles (WG, 198). Priestcraft is the dominion that the clergy has usurped over mind by pretending to have exclusive possession of the means of grace. In fact, prayer, churchgoing, baptism and communion are formalities that serve as schemata for moral duties (WG, 209).

What of belief in an afterlife of reward and punishment? Surprisingly, Kant tells us that faith in heaven and hell automatically imposes itself upon everyone. This is by virtue of the universal moral disposition in human nature. None the less, the gospel promises of recompense in the world to come are not meant to make this a motive for moral behaviour. Fear, in this life or for the next, is equally unworthy as a motive, and must not be imposed by religious officials. To take another being's life because of his faith is certainly wrong, unless a divine will has been made clear to the inquisitor, and that is something which can never be certain. Anyone who says 'whoever does not believe in this dogma is damned' must be ready to say 'if what I am telling you now is not true, let me be damned' (WG, 206).

14

The *Metaphysics of Morals*

In 1786 Frederick the Great was succeeded as King of Prussia by Frederick William II. The new monarch was keenly interested in religion, and when in 1794 he read Kant's *Religion within the Boundaries of Mere Reason* he was shocked. He claimed that the book misrepresented and undervalued many fundamental features of biblical Christianity. Kant refused to retract his opinions and denied he had been disparaging religion in his lectures. But he wrote to the King: 'As your Majesty's loyal subject I will hereafter refrain altogether from discoursing publicly, in lectures or in writings, on religion, whether natural or revealed.'

He turned his attention instead to international politics. Frederick William had taken part in the first coalition of states warring against Napoleon, but in 1795 he withdrew from it. Kant took this as a cue to write a brief treatise *Toward Perpetual Peace*. The centrepiece of the book is a set of definitive articles for perpetual peace. The articles run as follows:

1 The civil constitution in every state shall be republican.
2 The right of nations shall be based on a federalism of free states.
3 The citizen of any state shall have the right to visit any other state.

The first article seems surprising, given Kant's loyalty to the Prussian monarchy and his admiration for Frederick the Great. But Kant explains that republicanism is not the same as democracy: its essence is the separation between the executive and the legislature. The opposite of republicanism is despotism, and democracy itself can be despotic unless it is based on a representative system. Frederick II, he recalls, at least *said* he was only the highest servant of the state.

The reason, however, that Kant gives for the connection between republicanism and peace seems to depend on a republic being at least a representative democracy. When the citizens of a state have to give their consent in order to decide whether there shall be war or not, they will be very hesitant, Kant says, to begin such a bad game, since they will have to take upon themselves all the hardships of war.

The federalism of free states envisaged in the second article is something for the distant future: 'If good fortune should ordain that a powerful and enlightened people can form itself into a republic (which by its nature must be inclined to perpetual peace) this would provide a focal point of federative union for other states' (GM, 327).

It is interesting that the sedentary Kant should, in his third article, attach such importance to the free movement of citizens between states. But in his presentation of the article he makes clear that what he has in mind is to make a distinction between tourism and colonization. He denounces the horrifying lengths to which civilized, and especially commercial, states go when they visit foreign lands for the purpose of conquering them.

Kant prefaces his statement of principles with a number of practical first steps towards the distant goal of perpetual peace. Any treaty of peace must be more than a mere armistice. No independent state should be acquired by another through inheritance, exchange, purchase or donation. Standing armies should be abolished. No state should forcibly interfere in the constitution and government of another state. As long as wars continue, states should avoid using stratagems which will make trust impossible after hostilities end – he gives as examples assassination on the one hand, and the breach of terms of surrender on the other.

What guarantee can we have that perpetual peace will ever be achieved? Kant, who is usually so pessimistic, holds out the optimistic idea that nature will in the long term secure nations against violence and war by means of their mutual self-interest: 'It is the spirit of commerce, which cannot coexist with war and which sooner or later takes hold of every nation' (GM, 306–7). The power of money is the most reliable incentive to promote peace among nations, and to prevent war by mediation.

When writing his *Groundwork* Kant promised that he would follow it with a more expansive treatment of the metaphysic of morals. It was not until 1797 that a book of that title appeared; when it did it was something of a disappointment, and many of its early readers found it incoherent. But it contains much material of interest.

The introduction repeated a number of theses that had already been enunciated in the *Groundwork* and in the second *Critique*. Moral laws, Kant tells us at the start, need a necessary *a priori* basis, and cannot be learned from experience. Moral laws command for everyone in so far as he is free and has practical reason. It is a duty to have a metaphysic of morals (GM, 371). Pure reason does not contain the matter of the law, only the form, 'the fitness of maxims of choice to be universal law'. A maxim is a principle that the agent makes his own. Laws proceed from the will, maxims from choice: only choice is free. The greater the obstacles to be overcome, the more merit there is in a good deed (GM, 382). In lawgiving there are two elements: the action required, and the incentive. In ethical lawgiving the incentive is duty; in juridical lawgiving it includes other things such as punishment. All duties are either duties of right or duties of virtue; external lawgiving is possible only for the first. There is only one innate right: freedom from constraint by another's choice.

On this basis Kant develops the two parts of his treatise: the metaphysical elements of the theory of right, and the metaphysical elements of the theory of virtue. In the first he treats of property rights, domestic rights and contract rights. He also treats of public right – that is, the rights of the state and its officers. This part contains a firm statement that there can be no right to rebellion, and that anyone who attacks the person of a monarch should suffer the death penalty. A long footnote makes some attempt to reconcile this with Kant's initial enthusiasm for the French Revolution. 'Once a revolution has succeeded and a new constitution has been established, the lack of legitimacy with which it began and has been implemented cannot release the subjects from the obligation to comply with the new order of things' (GM, 465). Kant puts the question whether other powers have the right to band together in an alliance on behalf of a deposed monarch; but he leaves the question unanswered.

Kant is a convinced supporter of the death penalty. If a man has committed murder he must die; there is no substitute that will satisfy justice. If a civil society, for instance a republic on a small island, were to dissolve itself, before the citizens dispersed the last murderer remaining in prison would first have to be executed.

Kant allows that there are two cases where the death penalty for homicide is not necessary. The first is a duel in which
one officer kills another; the second is where a mother kills
her illegitimate child. His reason for clemency in this case
is even more horrifying than his rigour in other cases: 'A
child that comes into the world apart from marriage is born
outside the law and therefore outside the protection of the
law. It has, as it were, stolen into the commonwealth like
contraband merchandise' (GM, 477).

Kant discusses the rights and duties of states in relation to
war: their right to go to war, their right in war and their rights
after war. He admits now that perpetual peace, the ultimate
goal of the whole right of nations, is an unachievable idea –
but he says that political principles directed towards such an
end are not unachievable and are in fact obligatory. We must
act as if perpetual peace is a real possibility, even if it is not,
and we must work towards establishing it

In the *Metaphysical first principles of the doctrine of virtue*
Kant treats of one's duties towards oneself and towards the
happiness of others. A duty to love other beings he regards
as an absurdity because love is a matter of feeling, not living.
But to do good to other human beings in so far as we can is
a duty, whether one loves them or not. Lying is prohibited
not because of the harm it may do to others but because it
is the greatest violation of a person's duty to himself. 'By a
lie a human being throws away, and, as it were, annihilates
his dignity as a human being' (GM, 553). Kant is willing
to allow that untruths uttered from politeness need not be
considered as lies – but he insists that one must be held
responsible if evil consequences follow.

Kant discusses a number of character traits that have
appeared in lists of virtues and vices since the days of

Aristotle: avarice, servility, gratitude, sympathy, hatred, respect, arrogance. He concludes with a treatment of friendship. True friendship, it turns out, is an ideal unrealizable in practice, just like perpetual peace. But it is a practically necessary ideal, and to strive for friendship is a duty set by reason. What is possible, and indeed exists in isolated cases, is what Kant calls 'moral friendship' – namely 'the complete confidence of two persons in revealing their secret judgements and feelings to each other'.

When Kant wrote this he had already lost all but one of his personal friends and was on the point of quarrelling with his closest philosophical ally, Johann Gottlieb Fichte. Once Frederick William II died Kant felt free to publish on religion once more, and in 1798 he published his last work, *The Conflict of the Faculties,* which was based on three essays previously written but withheld from publication.

This work is really the complaint of a grumpy aged philosopher about the behaviour of members of the three higher faculties – theology, law and medicine. Kant sets out to tell them all how they should go about their business. Theologians should realize that the texts and systems that they deal with are contingent expressions of a single fundamental natural religion that is based not on any alleged revelation but on philosophical reason. Lawyers deal with the dictates and decrees of rulers of nation states constantly at war with each other; what they should really be concerned with is the progress of the human race towards an international republican system, exhibited in a crude and fragile way by the French Revolution. Doctors should be less concerned with drugs and surgery and more with reason's control over bodily processes through regimen and stoicism.

From 1799 Kant went into five years of slow decline. He lost weight, and found it hard to walk. His short-term memory departed and his sentences had to be finished for him by a sister who looked after him and whom he hardly recognized. He died in 1804, two months before his eightieth birthday, having made himself ill by overeating cheddar cheese sandwiches. His last words, as he sipped a glass of wine, were '*Es ist gut.*'

Part 2

THE LEGACY

15

Idealism and empiricism

In his last years Kant had begun to have misgivings about some aspects of the system of the first *Critique*, as is shown in his posthumously published papers. These were occasioned by criticisms aired by some of his own most devoted admirers and pupils, most notably by Fichte, who published his major philosophical work, *The Science of Knowledge*, in 1804, the year of Kant's death.

Fichte saw the task of philosophy in Kantian terms as providing a transcendental account of the possibility of experience. However, Kant's own system, so he believed, contained a radical inconsistency. Kant had never given up the notion that our experience was ultimately caused by 'things in themselves', even though we could know nothing about such things. But on his own account, the concept of cause was something that could only be applied within the sphere of phenomena. How then could there be an unknown, mind-independent cause outside this sphere?

Fichte tried to redesign Kant's system to remove the inconsistency. Two ways were possible. One would be to allow the notion of cause to extend beyond mere phenomena, and allow experience to be caused by things in themselves. That is the path of dogmatism. The other was to abandon the notion of a thing-in-itself and to say that experience is created by the thinking subject. This is the path of idealism, and that is the path that Fichte followed. He sought to prove that the whole of consciousness derived from the free experience of the thinking subject. Thus he made himself the uncompromising originator of German idealism.

The most famous and influential of German idealists was G. W. F. Hegel. Hegel's great contribution was to introduce a historical element into idealism. Whereas Fichte implausibly sought to account for the world as a product of individual consciousness, according to Hegel, cosmic history consists rather in the life story of Spirit (*Geist*). What then is Spirit? It is the opposite of matter, and while the essence of matter is gravity, the essence of Spirit is freedom. Freedom, for Hegel as for Kant, is at the apex of intelligible nature.

Hegel claims that the existence of Spirit is a matter of logic; but he uses the word 'logic' in a special sense of his own. Just as he sees history as a manifestation of logic, so he tends to see logic in historical, indeed martial, terms. If two propositions are contradictories, Hegel will describe this as a conflict between them: propositions do battle with one another and will emerge victorious or suffer defeat. In this process one proposition (the 'thesis') fights with another (the 'antithesis') and both are finally overcome by a third ('the synthesis'). Thus Hegel extends the apparatus of the antinomies of the first *Critique*, and christens it with the Kantian term 'dialectic'.

We pass through two stages of dialectic, we are told, in order to reach Spirit. We begin with the Absolute, the totality of reality, akin to the Being of earlier philosophers. Our first thesis is that the Absolute is pure Being. But pure Being without any qualities is nothing, so we are led to the antithesis, 'The Absolute is Nothing'. Thesis and antithesis are overcome by synthesis: the union of Being and Unbeing is Becoming, and so we say 'The Absolute is Becoming'.

Both Fichte and Hegel were German nationalists of a strident kind, at some distance from the cosmopolitan ideals of Kant's perpetual peace. The history of the world, according to Hegel, is the history of Spirit's ever-growing consciousness of its own freedom. Those who lived under oriental despots did not know that they were free beings. The Greeks and Romans knew that they themselves were free, but their acceptance of slavery showed that they did not know that man as such was free. 'The German nations, under the influence of Christianity, were the first to attain the consciousness that man, as man, is free: that it is the freedom of Spirit that constitutes its essence.'

Different states will have different characteristics corresponding to the Folk-spirit of the nation which they incorporate. At different times different Folk-spirits will be the primary manifestation of the progress of the World-spirit, and the people to which this primary manifestation belongs will be, for one epoch, the dominant people in the world. For each nation, the hour strikes once and only once, and Hegel believed that in his time the hour had struck for the German nation. The Prussian monarchy was the nearest thing on earth to the realization of an ideal state.

It was indeed in Germany that the influence of idealism was most strongly felt. In Britain in the early nineteenth century, the empiricist tradition carried on as if unaware that its foundations had been undermined by Kant. John Stuart Mill carried empiricism to extreme lengths. He defined matter as a permanent possibility of sensation, and claimed that the external world was no more than 'the world of possible sensations succeeding one another according to laws'. He went so far as to claim that mathematics was an *a posteriori* discipline: the truths of arithmetic were no more than very well-supported empirical generalizations.

In ethics Mill was a follower of Jeremy Bentham, the guiding idea of whose system was 'the principle of utility' or 'the greatest happiness of the greatest number'. The principle of utility evaluates every action according to the tendency which it appears to have to augment or diminish the general happiness. Utilitarianism stands at the opposite pole to the Kantian principle that duty is the overarching ethical principle, and that actions done to promote happiness are in themselves morally worthless.

Mill modified utilitarianism in some ways, but on the question of motivation he remains firmly on the side of Bentham vs Kant:

> He who saves a fellow-creature from drowning does what is morally right, whether his motive be duty or the hope of being paid for his trouble; he who betrays the friend that trusts him is guilty of a crime, even if his object be to serve another friend to whom he is under a greater obligation.

'The motive has nothing to do with the morality of the action, though much with the worth of an agent.'

Towards the end of the nineteenth century, British philosophy for a while fell under the influence of German idealism. After the death of John Stuart Mill a reaction had set in against the tradition of British empiricism of which he had been such a distinguished exponent. In 1874, a year after Mill's death, Oxford tutor T. H. Green (1836–82) brought out an edition of Hume's *Treatise of Human Nature* with a substantial introduction that subjected the presuppositions of empiricism to devastating criticism. In the same year there appeared the first of a long series of English translations of the works of

Hegel, which had first been introduced to Oxford in the 1840s by Benjamin Jowett (1817–93), the Master of Green's college, Balliol. Two years later F. H. Bradley of Merton published *Ethical Studies*, a founding classic of British Hegelianism. In 1893 Bradley completed *Appearance and Reality*, the fullest and most magisterial statement of British idealism. Shortly afterwards at Cambridge the methods and some of the doctrines of Hegel's *Logic* were expounded in a series of treatises by the Trinity College philosopher, J. M. E. McTaggart.

In Britain, however, the triumph of idealism was short-lived, and in the 1930s there was imported from the German-speaking world a particularly aggressive form of empiricism, namely the logical positivism of the Vienna Circle. Knowledge about the world, the Circle told us, could be gained only by experience, and propositions had meaning only if they could be either verified or falsified by experience. The thesis that the meaning of a proposition was the mode of its verification, the Verification Principle, was used to launch a massive attack on metaphysics. If two metaphysicians disputed over the nature of the Absolute, or the purpose of the Universe, they could be silenced by the question 'What possible experience would settle the issue between you?'

Although, in the nineteenth century, many thinkers were influenced by Kant in various ways, no philosopher of comparable stature arose to continue his philosophical project and to remedy its deficiencies. It was only in the twentieth century that a philosopher arrived possessed of the requisite genius: Ludwig Wittgenstein. In the following chapters I will try to set out the ways in which Wittgenstein was able to improve upon the Kantian system, and the extent to which Kant's insights remain valid in a post-Wittgensteinian philosophical world.

16

Logic and epistemology

One of Kant's innovations that has been very widely adopted is the distinction between analytic statements (where the predicate is contained in the subject) and synthetic statements (where that is not so). So too has the distinction he used between *a posteriori* statements (which can be known to be true only through experience) and *a priori* statements (knowable prior to experience). As we have seen, he attached great importance to the category of synthetic *a priori* statements, of which he gave arithmetic and geometry as examples. Similar such statements, he believed, were essential if metaphysics was to be possible.

The distinction between analytic and synthetic was subject to a famous attack in 1951 in an article entitled 'Two Dogmas of Empiricism' by the American philosopher W. V. O. Quine, himself an arch-empiricist. Quine sought to undermine this distinction, replacing it with a continuum of propositions of varying degrees of entrenchment in the web of our beliefs. He denied that any satisfactory definition could be given of analyticity, and he rejected the idea that a sentence was synthetic if it could be verified or falsified by experience. It is not single sentences, he argued, but whole systems – which include mathematics and logic as well as geography and history – that are verified or falsified: 'Our statements about the external world face the tribunal of sense experience not individually but only as a corporate body.' We cannot single out a class of analytic statements which remain true whatever happens; no statement can be totally immune to revision. Quine's attack received a robust response from the British philosophers Peter Strawson and W. G. Grice, and in spite of his criticisms the analytic/synthetic distinction seems to be still widely used.

I believe that Kant was fundamentally right to say that there are such things as synthetic *a priori* truths, and that they play a fundamental role in philosophy. But the logical and scientific context in which he employed his distinctions and enunciated this thesis has changed dramatically in the two centuries since his death. For Kant, Aristotelian logic and Euclidean geometry were permanent and unchallengeable disciplines. But in the nineteenth century mathematicians developed consistent non-Euclidean geometries and the philosopher Gottlob Frege invented a mathematical logic which superseded the Aristotelian syllogistic.

These innovations cast doubt on Kant's claim that arithmetic and geometry provided examples of synthetic *a priori* propositions. Geometry indeed remained synthetic, but ceased to be *a priori* – at least, it became a matter of scientific inquiry to discover which of the rival geometries was true of the actual world. Arithmetic, according to Frege, remained *a priori* but could be shown to be analytic. Not only did he show how to conduct logic in a mathematical manner, he claimed that arithmetic itself could be proved to be a branch of logic, in the sense that it could be formalized without the use of any non-logical notions or axioms. This thesis became known as 'logicism'.

Frege's most important step was to define arithmetical notions, such as that of number, in terms of purely logical notions, such as that of class. He achieved this by treating the cardinal numbers as classes of equivalent classes, that is to say, of classes with the same number of members. Thus the number two is the class of pairs, and the number three the class of trios. Such a definition at first sight appears circular, but in fact it is not since the notion of equivalence between classes can be defined without making use of the notion of number. Two classes are equivalent to each other if they can be mapped onto each other without residue. Thus, to take an example of Frege's, a waiter may know that there are as many knives as there are plates on a table without knowing how many of each there are. All he needs to do is to observe that there is a knife to the right of every plate and a plate to the left of every knife.

Thus, we could define four as the class of all classes equivalent to the class of Gospel makers. But such a defin-ition would be useless for the logicist's purpose since the fact that there were four Gospel makers is no part of logic. Frege has to find, for each number, not only a class of the right size, but one whose size is guaranteed by logic. He does this by beginning with zero as the first of the num-ber series. This can be defined in purely logical terms as the class of all classes equivalent to the class of objects that are not identical with themselves: a class which obviously has no members ('the null class'). We can then go on to define the number one as the class of all classes equivalent to the class whose only member is zero. In order to pass from these definitions to definitions of the other natural numbers, Frege also offers a definition of the notion of 'suc-ceeding' in the sense in which three succeeds two, and four succeeds three, in the number series. With the aid of this definition the other numbers can be defined without using any notions other than logical ones such as identity, class, and class equivalence. And if Frege's derivation of arithmetic from logic is successful, then its statements are analytic, and not synthetic as Kant believed.

Frege aimed to present his derivation of arithmetic in two massive volumes. However, his ambitious project was aborted before he could complete it. Before the publication of his second volume in 1903, he received a letter from an English philosopher, Bertrand Russell, pointing out that the system of logic on which the derivation was based was in fact inconsistent. The system permitted without restriction the formation of classes of classes, and classes of classes of classes, and so on. Classes must themselves be classifiable. Now can a class be a member of itself? Most classes are not (the class of men is not a man) but some apparently are (e.g. the class of classes is surely a class). It seems, therefore, that we have two kinds of classes: those that are members of themselves and those that are not. But the formation of the class of all classes that are not members of themselves leads to paradox: if it is a member of itself, then it is not a member of itself, and if it is not a member of itself, then it is a member of itself. A system which leads to such a paradox cannot be logically sound.

It turns out that the path from the axioms of logic via the axioms of arithmetic to the theorems of arithmetic is barred at two points. Not only, as Russell showed, was the theory of classes that was part of Frege's logical basis inconsistent in itself. Later on the notion of 'axioms of arithmetic' was itself called in question when it was shown (by the Austrian mathematician Kurt Gödel in 1931) that it was impossible to give arithmetic itself a complete and consistent axiomatization. By the time of his death Frege returned to the Kantian view that arithmetic is synthetic *a priori*.

Wittgenstein, like Frege, eventually accepted a position close to that of Kant. That the propositions of mathematics are synthetic, he said, is brought out by the fact that the occurrence of prime numbers in the number sequence is unpredictable. He was even willing to speak of synthetic *a priori* propositions, though in a sense rather different from Kant's.

More interestingly, towards the end of his life Wittgenstein sought to clarify the status of a set of propositions which have a special position in the structure of our epistemology, propositions which, as he put it, 'stand fast' for us. Propositions such as 'Mont Blanc has existed for a long time' or 'one cannot fly to the moon by flapping one's arms' look like empirical propositions. But they are not the results of inquiry, but the foundations of research: they are fossilized empirical propositions which form channels for the ordinary, fluid propositions. They are propositions that make up our world-picture, and a world-picture is not learnt by experience; it is the inherited background against which I distinguish between true and false. Children do not learn such propositions; they as it were swallow them down with what they do learn.

For example, it is quite certain that motor cars don't grow out of the earth. If someone could believe the contrary he could believe *everything* we say is untrue, and would question our whole system of verification. Propositions such as that are not the result of learning and experience, but they have to be true if it is to be possible for us to make sense of experience at all. In that respect, they closely resemble Kant's synthetic *a priori* propositions. Only, rather in the spirit of Quine, Wittgenstein insists: When we first begin to believe anything, we believe not a single proposition but a whole system: light dawns gradually over the whole.

17

From physics to metaphysics

In his treatment of the theoretical powers of the human mind Kant brings four cognitive faculties into play: the senses, the intellect, the judgement and the reason. In this chapter I wish to ask how far Kant was correct to identify and distinguish these faculties, and how accurately or inaccurately he describes their functioning.

A distinction between the senses and the intellect was made long ago by Plato and Aristotle, and has never been totally absent from the history of philosophy. However, in the period between Descartes and Kant, rationalists exaggerated the role of the intellect and empiricists exaggerated the scope of the senses. Kant was surely correct to emphasize that, in an adult human, both powers are to be involved if any knowledge is to be achieved. We must continue to accept his thesis that without the senses no objects are given to us and that without intellect no object would be thought. We can endorse his dictum 'Thoughts without content are empty, awareness without concepts is blind.'

Kant accepted the traditional view of the senses as passive, and neglected the exploratory character of our sensibility. His special contribution in this area was the claim of the transcendental aesthetic that space and time were *a priori* forms of sensory awareness. We saw in the last chapter that nineteenth-century developments in logic and mathematics seemed initially to call into question Kant's theory of the synthetic *a priori*. In the case of the transcendental aesthetic, on the other hand, twentieth-century developments in physics seemed to go some way to support his account of space and time.

According to Einstein's theory of special relativity there is no absolute measure of simultaneity, and therefore no absolute ordering of objects in time. An event A may appear to precede an event B when observed by an observer C travelling at a certain speed in a certain position; to an observer D in a different position travelling at a different speed, B may appear to precede A. Space and time therefore are not the absolutes that they initially appear. Special relativity may perhaps be looked at as a precise mathematical formulation of Kant's intuition that they were *a priori* forms of awareness. Or, more plausibly, we may attribute to Kant a loosening of our naïve notions of space and time that made room for later conceptual developments.

Science makes progress through hypothesis and experiment, through collaboration between the intellect and the senses. The special light that Kant throws on the progress of science is shown in the *Critique of the Power of Judgment*, where he stresses the aesthetic and teleological element in the scientific project. In their explanations, scientists seek not only truth, but also simplicity and unity. Viewing nature as a single whole is itself something that goes beyond naked empirical evidence.

In the early twentieth century, the scientific orthodoxy was very distant from Kant's understanding of nature as a teleological system in which organic wholes were both the effect and the cause of their parts. There was a broad consensus that the sciences formed a hierarchy in which each level was to be explained in terms of the one below it. Psychology was to be explained by physiology, physiology by chemistry, and chemistry by physics. This scientific strategy was called 'reductionism', since all sciences were ultimately to be reduced to physics.

Reductionist science chalked up victory after victory, as more and more lower-level mechanisms were discovered to explain higher-level processes. For instance, the pacemaker rhythm of the heart was explained in terms of the flow of ions of potassium and calcium through protein channels. However, further investigation showed that in the heartbeat there was not only upward causation from the molecular level to the cellular level but also downward causation from the cell influencing the molecules. It is nowadays clear that in biology there is no privileged level of causation. Living organisms are multi-level open systems in which the behaviour at any level depends on higher and lower levels and cannot be fully understood in isolation.

One of the goals of reductionism was to eliminate from science all teleology or goal-directedness. In fact, teleology is ubiquitous in nature. However, it operates in different ways at different levels. At the purely molecular level the protein-membrane network that sustains cardiac rhythm has no goal: its function only becomes clear at the level of cells. In its turn, the cellular activity serves a purpose that only emerges at the still higher level of the cardiovascular system. There is not only bottom-up causation, but top-down causation; as Kant realised when he said that there were descending as well as ascending series of causal dependency.

At least in biology, today's understanding of the structure of nature is closer to Kant's exposition in the third *Critique* than it is to the reductionist theorizing of the early twentieth

century. Is the same true of the relationship between intellect and reason which was the subject of the first *Critique*?

The target of that *Critique* was pure reason, that is to
say the use of the intellect divorced from experience. Pure
reason, in its quest for an absolute reality, in fact produces
nothing other than illusion, the deliverances of traditional
metaphysics. The illusory nature of these dogmatic theses is
exposed by Kant in his dialectic.

Wittgenstein, like Kant, was an enemy of dogmatic metaphysics. And like Kant, he saw the source of such illusory
dogmas in a blurring of the distinction between science
and philosophy. In the view of both these philosophers, the
metaphysician is a philosopher who is deceiving himself
that he is a scientist. 'Philosophy is not one of the natural
sciences,' Wittgenstein wrote in the *Tractatus*. Scientism,
that is the attempt to see philosophy as a science, was his
bête noire. In the *Blue Book* he wrote: 'Philosophers constantly see the methods of science before their eyes, and are
irresistibly tempted to answer questions in the way science
does. This tendency is the real source of metaphysics, and
leads the philosopher into complete darkness.'

For Wittgenstein science and philosophy are two totally
different activities, science being concerned with information and explanation, philosophy with description and
understanding. Philosophy is not a body of doctrine but an
activity of clarification. It is not a matter of acquiring new
truths about the world; the philosopher is not in possession
of information that is denied to others. Philosophy is not a
matter of knowledge, it is a matter of understanding, that is
to say, of organizing what is known.

Wittgenstein's account of the nature of philosophy looks
on the surface rather different from Kant's because it is

expressed in linguistic terms. He sees the human mind as essentially the ability to learn and use language in all the variety of its forms. Kant did not explicitly endorse this view, but it is implicit in everything he writes – for instance his understanding of concepts and judgements in terms of grammatical subjects and grammatical predicates. It was left to Wittgenstein to make explicit the link between mind and language, and to explore in much greater detail than Kant ever did the variety of forms of language and their embedding in life and social behaviour.

The element of Kant's philosophy that is most difficult to endorse today is his belief in the thing-in-itself. Within his own system it is difficult to make out whether he believes that each object contains a thing in itself – so that there would be a Napoleon-*an-sich* – or whether it is just that at the heart of the universe there is an unknowable residue of fact. We may agree with Fichte that it may well be best to dispense altogether with this feature of the Kantian system. The only way to make sense of it is to regard it as an injunction never to give up on the scientific quest: however much we learn about nature, there is always more to be learned.

18

Freedom and morality

In several places Kant offers the following argument. The moral law places obligations on us. But we can be obliged to do only what is in our power to do. Hence we must possess the freedom to carry out our duty. By means of this argument, he claims, practical reason restores to us the freedom that was one of the great objects of metaphysics, and of which we seemed to be deprived by the critique of theoretical reason.

His argument has convinced few people. 'Ought implies can' is correct if it means that it is unreasonable to impose on anyone an obligation that she is incapable of fulfilling. But in Kant's system it means that an intolerable burden of duty must presuppose a transcendental freedom of the will. In his more gentle moments Kant is willing to say such things as that there is no duty to take beer rather than wine, or wine rather than beer, with one's dinner. But his official line is that at every moment one has the duty to do the maximum possible amount of good.

The freedom which Kant presupposes as a necessary condition for the fulfilment of duty is not a freedom within the world of appearances. It is a freedom which belongs to the agent as a noumenal entity outside time, not a phenomenal person situated in the everyday world. It is impossible to see how, in that case, our free actions can have effects in the sensory world. But if they cannot, then it must be delusory to call them free.

Nonetheless I believe that Kant was in the right to say that intellectual freedom is compatible with physical determinism. We should replace his distinction between the noumenal and phenomenal agent with a distinction between a human being considered as an intelligent agent and as a physical organism. An agent could be free at the level of practical reasoning even if it were true that as a material entity its movements were determined by the laws of physics. If physics offers the most basic level of explanation, and physics is determinist, that does not mean that voluntariness at the level of animal behaviour, and intention at the level of human behaviour, are mere illusions.

'Freedom of the will', it must be admitted, is an unfortunate expression. The will is a capacity, and a capacity cannot be free. Only persons and actions can be free. But what people mean by the expression is that human beings have a capacity for free action. Some analyses of freedom lay most emphasis on the notion of choice or desire, others lay most emphasis on the notion of ability or power. Some define free will as the capacity to do what one wants, others define it as the power of action in the face of alternatives. On the one account, a person does something freely if he does it because he wants to; on the other account he does something freely if he does it though it is in his power not to do it.

Each of these two concepts of freedom is inseparably linked with the other. The type of power to do otherwise which is necessary for freedom is the power to do otherwise if one wants to. Mere indeterminacy or randomness, such as that of elementary particles in quantum jumps, does not amount to anything like free will. On the other hand, it cannot be true that one acted because one wanted to unless one had in some measure and at some point the possibility of acting otherwise than one did. The two kinds of freedom are two sides of the same coin.

Freedom undoubtedly involves the power to do otherwise. I do X freely only if I have the power not to do X. This power has two elements: the ability not to do X and the opportunity not to do X. The truth that is misleadingly presented under the rubric 'freedom of the will' is that human beings very often do one thing when they have the ability and the opportunity to do otherwise. And it is possible to ascertain the presence of these abilities and opportunities without knowing anything about whatever events may be taking place in the imagination or the brain of the free agent.

This shows that human freedom is compatible with physical, and indeed physiological, determinism. But of course there is no reason to believe that our actions are determined by physics, or that physics itself is determinist. In fact it is the stochastic nature of the lowest level of explanation which makes it possible for systems at a higher level to control those at a lower level in the manner that Kant, as we have seen in the previous chapter, foresaw.

Kant described God, freedom and immortality as postulates of practical reason. He was wrong about each of them, but the actual notion of a postulate of practical reason retains its value. Such a postulate was something that had to be assumed, prior to any evidence, if we were to make sense of our moral obligations. There is nothing incoherent in such a concept, and indeed we frequently use them. For instance, policies relating to gender may well be based on the assumption that in a perfectly fair world men and women would be equally represented at all levels of competence and authority. That assumption is a postulate of practical reason; it cannot be based on experience since there has never been a perfectly fair world.

Another feature of Kant's moral system that retains its validity is the idea of an autonomous moral community that draws up laws for itself. There are three elements that are essential to morality: a moral community, a set of moral values, and a moral code. All three are necessary. First, it is as impossible to have a purely private morality as it is to have a purely private language, and for very similar reasons. Second, the moral life of the community consists in the shared pursuit of non-material values, such as fairness, truth, comradeship, freedom. It is the nature of the values pursued that distinguishes morality from economics. Third, this pursuit is carried out within a framework which excludes certain prohibited types of behaviour. It is this that distinguished morality from aesthetics, which is also a pursuit of non-material values. If we ask the question 'Who does the prohibiting?' the answer is that it is the members of the moral community. The moral community creates moral laws in a manner similar to that in which the linguistic community creates the rules of grammar and syntax. Moral rules, like linguistic rules, may change as society changes; but unless a set of such rules is in operation society collapses into anarchy as language collapses into incoherence.

This conception of the origin of moral rules was picturesquely sketched by Kant in the notion of the kingdom of ends, a union of rational beings under common laws. My own will is rational only in so far as its maxims – the principles on which it makes its choices – are capable of being made universal laws. The converse of this is that universal law is law that is made by rational wills like mine. A rational being is 'subject only to laws which are made by himself and yet are universal'. In the kingdom of ends, we are all both legislators and subjects.

19

Religion and politics

How well have Kant's theses about religion stood the test of time? We can pose the question separately in relation to three separate facets of his thought: his critique of the proofs of God's existence; his account of the relationship between religion and morality; and his exposition of the meaning of Christian doctrine.

Kant objected to the ontological argument on the grounds that existence is not a predicate. I believe that his criticism is sound, but it must be admitted that in recent years a sophisticated defence of the argument has been mounted. The Templeton-Prize-winning philosopher Alvin Plantinga begins his version of the argument by defining the property of maximal excellence, a property that includes omniscience, omnipotence and moral perfection. Obviously God, if he exists, has maximal excellence in the actual world. But maximal excellence is not sufficient for Godhead: we need to consider worlds other than this one. Maximal greatness, we may say, is maximal excellence in every possible world, and it is that which is the mark of divinity. Now anything which possesses maximal greatness must exist in every possible world, because in a world in which a thing does not exist it does not possess any properties. If maximal greatness is instantiated, then it is instantiated in every world. If so, then it is instantiated in our world, the actual world: that is to say, Godhead is instantiated and God exists.

Plantinga's argument, like earlier versions of the ontological argument, takes us from a concept of God – in this case, the maximally great being – to the existence of God, that is to say the instantiation of God in the actual world. It presupposes that the notion of maximal greatness is a possible one, and that in turn supposes that the whole apparatus of possible worlds is coherent and that we can conceive of one and the same individual existing in more than one possible world. This is doubted, for good reason, by many philosophers. However, it is not a premise that Kant himself can reject, because in his own treatment of the ontological argument he imagines a merely possible Julius Caesar possessing all the properties that the actual Julius Caesar possessed in the real world.

The argument for God's existence that Kant treats with most respect in his mature work is the argument from design, which he calls the physico-theological proof. The reputation of this argument suffered a severe shock when Darwin proposed the theory of evolution by natural selection. Structures and behaviours which it once seemed obvious to assign to intelligent design could, after Darwin, be explained by purely biological factors. The argument that the adaptation of organisms to their environment exhibits the handiwork of a benevolent creator has accordingly lost much of its attraction.

On the other hand, it is wrong to suggest, as is often done, that Darwin disproved the existence of God. For all Darwin showed, the whole machinery of natural selection may have been part of a Creator's design for the universe. After all, belief that we humans are God's creatures has never been regarded as incompatible with our being the children of our parents; it is no more incompatible with us being, on both sides, descended from the ancestors of the apes.

In fact the only argument refuted by Darwin would be one which said: Wherever there is adaptation to environment we must see the immediate activity of an intelligent being. But the physico-theological proof did not claim this, and Kant repeatedly emphasized that one should not invoke the direct input of a creative intelligence in cases where the natural properties of created substances provided a sufficient explanation. The argument was only that the ultimate explanation of such properties and of their adaptation must be found in intelligence. If the argument was ever sound, then the success of Darwinism merely inserts an extra step between the phenomena to be explained and their ultimate explanation.

Many religious people, as well as secular non-believers, will nowadays agree with Kant that it is a mistake to see moral rules as originating in divine commands. Indeed, contemporary expositions of Kantian moral teaching often go much further than Kant in making a separation between morality and religion. Kant's conception of the kingdom of ends made a place for God as the one person who was a legislator without being a subject. Nowadays this element of his system is often tacitly dropped, and the kingdom of ends becomes a republic of ends.

In attempting to reinterpret, or explain away, the more difficult features of Christian doctrine and practice, Kant has had many followers even among the devout. But few have been attracted by his strategy of reducing the Creed to an inculcation of the demands of an overarching, unrelenting call of duty. When the demythologization of *Religion within the Boundaries of Mere Reason* has been completed it is hard to see what is left that can be called Christianity. Kant put his position bluntly in a letter to a friend in 1775:

> The true doctrine coincides with a purely moral faith that God will support all our genuine efforts at doing good, even if their success may not be in our power. The adulation of the teacher of this religion (Jesus) as well as the asking for favors in prayer and devotion is inessential.

In recent years political scientists and students of international relations have been taking a keen interest in Kant's late work on perpetual peace. There has been a spate of articles on 'the Kantian tripod' debating whether it is correct to say that democracy, economic interdependence and involvement in international organizations reduce the incidence of wars (or, as they are called by the professionals, 'militarized international disputes'). Sophisticated statistical techniques, using data from more than one century, seek to identify the variables and factors responsible for the outbreaks of conflict between nations. It is difficult for the philosophical student of Kant to evaluate the regressions offered on the two sides of these debates, which seem to take no account of Kant's sharp distinction between republics and democracies. But the very existence of the debates is testimony to the continuing power of Kant's genius.

Kant's political thought shares a structure with his epistemological and moral thought. In each case he holds up an ideal which we will never achieve, but towards which all our striving must be directed – in epistemology, knowledge of things in themselves; in morality, perfect submission to duty; in politics perpetual peace. In mathematics an asymptote is a line that continually approaches a given curve but never meets it. If we wanted a single word to describe the structure of Kant's thinking it would be 'asymptotic'.

Glossary

a posteriori   based on experience
a priori   prior to experience
aesthetic   (1) concerning the senses; (2) concerning beauty
analytic statement whose predicate is contained in its subject
analytic v. dialectic   constructive v. destructive part of philosophy
apperception   self-awareness
autonomy self-government
awareness (*Anschauung*)   experience
categorical   unconditional
cosmological argument   argument drawn from the nature of the world
disjunctive   'either … or' statement.
duty   the supreme moral motive
heteronomy   government by something other than oneself
hypothetical   dependent on an 'if'
intellect (*Verstand*)   the faculty of thinking
judgement   mental act corresponding to a statement
maxim   a principle of action adopted by an agent
noumena   objects of pure reason
ontological argument   argument based on what is meant by 'God'
paralogism   fallacious reasoning
phenomena   appearances
physico-theology   argument to God from design
positing   stating existence

principle   rule of action

reason (*Vernunft*)   most ambitious intellectual power

sensory   concerned with the senses

synthetic   containing a predicate not already included in a subject

teleology   purposiveness

transcendental   beyond the scope of experience

Further reading

Beck, Lewis White, *A Commentary on Kant's Critique of Practical Reason* (Chicago: Chicago UP, 1960).

Bennett, Jonathan, *Kant's Analytic* (Cambridge: CUP, 1966).

Bennett, Jonathan, *Kant's Dialectic* (Cambridge: CUP, 1974).

Cassirer, Ernst, *Kant's Life and Thought* (New Haven: Yale UP, 1981).

Guyer, Paul, *Kant and the Claims of Knowledge* (Cambridge: CUP, 1987).

Guyer, Paul, *Kant and the Claims of Taste* (Cambridge, MA: Harvard UP, 1979).

Guyer, Paul, ed., *The Cambridge Companion to Kant* (Cambridge: CUP, 1992).

Hare, John E., *God and Morality* (Oxford: Blackwell, 2007).

Kanterian, E., *Kant, God, and Metaphysics: The Secret Thorn* (London: Routledge, 2018)

Kemp Smith, Norman, *Critique of Pure Reason* (London: Macmillan, 1963).

Kitcher, Patricia, *Kant's Transcendental Psychology* (Oxford: OUP, 1990)

Körner, Stephan, *Kant* (London: Penguin, 1955).

Kuehn, Manfred, *Kant: A Biography* (Cambridge: CUP, 2001).

Noble, Denis, *Dance to the Tune of Life* (Cambridge: CUP, 2017).

O'Neill, Onora, *Constructions of Reason: Explorations of Kant's Practical Philosophy* (Cambridge: CUP, 1989).

Paton, H. J., *The Categorical Imperative* (London: Hutchinson, 1947).

Paton, H. J., *The Moral Law* (London: Hutchinson, 1948).

Reed, T. J., *Light in Germany* (Chicago: Chicago UP, 2015).

Strawson, P. F., *The Bounds of Sense* (London: Methuen, 1966).

Further reading

Walker, Ralph C. S., *Kant* (London: Routledge, 1978).

Ward, Keith, *The Development of Kant's View of Ethics* (Oxford: Blackwell, 1972).

Wood, Allen, *Kant's Rational Theology* (Ithaca, NY: Cornell UP, 1978).

Index

Index

Index

Index